The Language of Newspapers

This accessible satellite textbook in the Routledge INTERTEXT series is unique in offering students hands-on practical experience of textual analysis focused on newspapers. Written in a clear, user-friendly style by an experienced teacher, it combines practical activities with texts, accompanied by commentaries which show how newspapers present, create and influence aspects of our culture, and suggestions for further activities. It can be used individually or in conjunction with the series core textbook, *Working with Texts: A core book for language analysis*.

Aimed at A-Level and beginning undergraduate students, *The Language of Newspapers*:

- examines how the press is ideologically biased
- explores stylistic contrasts in the portrayal of current events
- includes numerous text examples from a range of broadsheets and tabloids, such as the birth of Madonna's baby, the divorce of Charles and Diana, and the Mandy Allwood case
- has a comprehensive glossary of terms

Danuta Reah is a co-author of *Working with Texts: A core book for language analysis*. She is a senior examiner for the NEAB English Language A Level and currently runs an educational consultancy.

The Intertext series

◎ **Why does the phrase 'spinning a yarn' refer both to using language and to making cloth?**

◎ **What might a piece of literary writing have in common with an advert or a note from the milkman?**

◎ **What aspects of language are important to understand when analysing texts?**

The Routledge INTERTEXT series will develop readers' understanding of how texts work. It does this by showing some of the designs and patterns in the language from which they are made, by placing texts within the contexts in which they occur, and by exploring relationships between them.

The series consists of a foundation text, *Working with Texts: A core book for language analysis*, which looks at language aspects essential for the analysis of texts, and a range of satellite texts. These apply aspects of language to a particular topic area in more detail. They complement the core text and can also be used alone, providing the user has the foundation skills furnished by the core text.

Benefits of using this series:

◎ **Unique** – written by a team of respected teachers and practitioners whose ideas and activities have also been trialled independently

◎ **Multi-disciplinary** – provides a foundation for the analysis of texts, supporting students who want to achieve a detailed focus on language

◎ **Accessible** – no previous knowledge of language analysis is assumed, just an interest in language use

◎ **Comprehensive** – wide coverage of different genres: literary texts, notes, memos, signs, advertisements, leaflets, speeches, conversation

◎ **Student-friendly** – contains suggestions for further reading; activities relating to texts studied; commentaries after activities; key terms highlighted and an index of terms

The series editors:

Ronald Carter is Professor of Modern English Language in the Department of English Studies at the University of Nottingham and is the editor of the Routledge INTERFACE series in Language and Literary Studies. He is also co-author of *The Routledge History of Literature in English*. From 1989 to 1992 he was seconded as National Director for the Language in the National Curriculum (LINC) project, directing a £21.4 million in-service teacher education programme.

Angela Goddard is Senior Lecturer in Language at the Centre for Human Communication, Manchester Metropolitan University, and was Chief Moderator for the Project element of English Language A-Level for the Northern Examination and Assessment Board (NEAB) from 1983 to 1995. Her publications include *The Language Awareness Project: Language and Gender*, vols I and II, 1988, and *Researching Language*, 1993 (Framework Press).

First series title:

Working with Texts: A core book for language analysis
Ronald Carter, Angela Goddard, Danuta Reah, Keith Sanger, Maggie Bowring

Satellite titles:

The Language of Sport
Adrian Beard

The Language of Advertising: Written Texts
Angela Goddard

The Language of Poetry
John McRae

The Language of Newspapers
Danuta Reah

The Language of Humour
Alison Ross

The Language of Fiction
Keith Sanger

Related titles:

INTERFACE series:

Variety in Written English
Tony Bex

Language, Literature and Critical Practice
David Birch

A Linguistic History of English Poetry
Richard Bradford

The Language of Jokes
Delia Chiaro

The Discourse of Advertising
Guy Cook

Literary Studies in Action
Alan Durant and Nigel Fabb

English in Speech and Writing
Rebecca Hughes

Feminist Stylistics
Sara Mills

Language in Popular Fiction
Walter Nash

Textual Intervention
Rob Pope

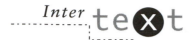

The Language of Newspapers

- Danuta Reah

LONDON AND NEW YORK

First published 1998
by Routledge
11 New Fetter Lane, London EC4P 4EE

Simultaneously published in the USA and
Canada
by Routledge
29 West 35th Street, New York, NY 10001

Typeset in Stone Sans/Stone Serif by
Solidus (Bristol) Limited

Printed and bound in Great Britain by TJ
International Ltd., Padstow, Cornwall

*British Library Cataloguing in Publication
Data*

A catalogue record for this book is
available from the British Library

*Library of Congress Cataloguing in Publication
Data*

Reah, Danuta, 1949–
      The language of newspapers/Danuta
Reah.
      p.   cm.

      ISBN 0–415–14600–3

      1.   English language – Discourse
analysis.   2.   Newspapers – Language.
      I.   Title.
PE1422.R43   1998
420. 1'41 – dc21

                                    97-17315
                                    CIP

contents

acknowledgements

Thank you to everyone who helped me with this book, especially Ken Reah, Alison Ross and Keith Sanger for reading and commenting on the drafts.

Thank you especially to Angela Goddard and Ron Carter for their invaluable editorial support and advice.

Finally, many thanks to the staff of the Sheffield Star for allowing me to visit their news room and answering my questions.

The following texts and illustrations have been reprinted by courtesy of their copyright holders:

Daily Telegraph

'Diana's fingers "do the talking" ', 29 August 1996.

The Sun

'Hula Meanie Spurns Sun Readers on Loot', 9 September 1996; 'Salute from the Poms', 20 January 1988; 'Long May She Rein!', 30 July 1996; 'A stunning pal . . .', 14 August 1996; ' "Killer" nurses must die, say angry family', 6 January 1997; 'Pervy Jerry's Poem of Love to Gay Boy', 6 January 1997; 'He is my man', 12 August 1996; ' "Quiz Them" call to cops', 12 August 1996; 'She's no longer my daughter says mum', 12 August 1996; 'Mandy's Tears for her 8 Tots', 15 October 1996; 'I got my 8 babies free from Boots', 12 August 1996; 'Madonna baby born', 15 October 1996; 'Gotcha', 4 May 1982.

Daily Mirror

'Queen Snubs 102,625 Daily Mirror Readers', 30 July 1996; 'I lay awake as docs cut me open', 15 October 1996; 'Street Maxine's Drive Ban Cut . . .', 15 October 1996; 'Victim weeps as stalking ex-love freed', 14 August 1996; 'Cindy's Nappy Ending', 15 October 1996; 'Glenda to fight on the beaches', 14 August 1996. All reproduced by permission of Mirror Syndication International.

Acknowledgements

Daily Mail

'What a Liberty', 28 October 1996; 'Four-letter TV Poem Fury', 12 October 1987; 'Pity little Lourdes', 16 October 1996: all reproduced by permission of Solo.

The Guardian

'Express chief's wife arrested on suspicion of stealing Fergie book', by Nick Varley, 14 November 1996; 'Eight miniature coffins ...', 15 October 1996: all reproduced by permission of The Guardian.

Daily Express

'Diana breaks taboo to upstage the Queen', 14 August 1996; 'Women wanted for building site work', 14 August 1996; 'Boy who dragged down a Tory MP', 6 January 1997; 'Revenge of the little mummy's boy', 6 January 1997.

The Independent

'Million-pound mum', 12 August 1996.

The Times

'Argentine cruiser hit by torpedoes from Royal Navy submarine', 4 May 1982. Reproduced by permission of © Times Newspapers Limited, 1982.

The publishers have made every effort to contact copyright holders although this has not been possible in some cases. Outstanding permissions will be remedied in future editions. Please contact the Textbook Development Editor at Routledge.

Introduction

Who wants yesterday's papers? Yesterday's newspaper is a useful metaphor for something that has lost its value. Yesterday's news isn't news at all. Old newspapers are used for wrapping chips, for wrapping rubbish, for making papier-mâché, for recycling and for throwing away.

This book is all about yesterday's papers, if only because any newspaper written about in this book will be yesterday's paper (or last year's paper) by the time this book is in print.

But it is also about yesterday's papers because they are important. They provide a series of snapshots of our life and our culture, often from a very specific viewpoint. This book is written to look at the way these texts present, and to a certain extent create or at least influence, aspects of our culture and society.

WHAT IS A NEWSPAPER?

The answer to this question seems at first to be so obvious that the question is hardly worth asking. However, it is a serious question, and one that must be addressed if the language of newspapers is to be looked at in any meaningful way.

For the purposes of this book, newspapers will be divided into three kinds: the broadsheet newspapers, that is, the *Telegraph*, the *Independent*, the *Times* and the *Guardian*; the middle-range tabloids, that is, the *Express* and the *Daily Mail*; and the tabloids, that is, the *Sun*, the *Mirror*, the *Star* (this classification is taken from Tunstall, 1996). There are obviously other newspapers that don't fit into this model, for example, local newspapers and newspapers of particular political groups such as the *Socialist Worker*. However, this book will look at the national British press.

The term *newspaper* suggests that the content of a newspaper will be primarily devoted to the news of the day, and some analysis and comment on this news. Newspapers, however, contain a range of items; news, comment and analysis, advertising, entertainment. In fact, the larger part of a newspaper will be devoted to items other than news, for example, TV listings and advertising. A percentage of the news stories will relate to the activities of celebrities, film and TV stars (particularly soap stars), and the activities of the royal family. Is this news?

Activity

Look at the content of one tabloid and one broadsheet newspaper. Classify the contents under the following headings (roughly, by number of pages or fractions of pages): news, sport and entertainment, advertising.

Now classify the news under the following headings: home news (i.e., stories about Britain or British people), overseas news.

Classify the home news into: stories about current events, political stories, stories about royalty, stories about other celebrities, other.

Commentary

An editor of the *New York Times* once said that about 60 per cent of the content of his newspaper was advertising. The papers you have looked at may not contain such a high percentage, but it is highly unlikely that the highest percentage of the paper is devoted to news coverage.

A similar analysis carried out on the *Sun* and the *Guardian* of Friday, 13 December 1996 gave the following figures (this analysis excludes magazines and pull-out sections, so the *Guardian*'s tabloid magazine is excluded, as is the *Sun*'s television guide):

2

Paper	Sun	Guardian
No. of pages	60	26
Pages of news	16.5 (28%)	12 (46%)
Pages of advertising	26 (43%)	8 (31%)
Sport and entertainment	17.5 (29%)	6 (23%)

An analysis of this kind clearly demonstrates that the major content of a newspaper is not its news reporting. The above analysis clearly shows that news stories are the greatest single item in the Guardian, but advertising is the greater element in the tabloid. This may be because the Guardian has a tabloid section that has not been included in this analysis. This section contains no news coverage, and if the advertising content of the tabloid had been included, then the percentage of advertising in the Guardian might have been higher. The main point is, however, that in both papers, sport, entertainment and advertising occupy a greater number of pages than does news, and the percentage of page space in both cases demonstrates the importance of advertising content to both papers.

A further point that you might have noticed is the extent to which stories about individuals — whether they are celebrities or not — dominate the news, rather than stories about issues. The section on representation of groups (Unit 4) will look at stories about, for example, the gay community that focus exclusively on individuals and the so-called scandal element, rather than looking at the more general problems and processes that these stories represent.

Newspapers are also artefacts of the commercial and political world. For example, before the break-up of the USSR, the pronounce-ments of the state newspaper *Pravda* were treated with scepticism by Western commentators, as *Pravda* was seen as the mouthpiece of the ruling Communist Party. It was assumed that even if the editor of *Pravda* wanted to oppose the party ideology he would not be allowed to.

The Western democracies, on the other hand, are seen as having a 'free press'. The freedom of the press is a matter of ideological impor-tance, and one that is enshrined, for example, in the US Constitution. This book is concerned with the British press, and examples and analyses will be taken from British newspapers. The British press, too, is seen as free, and though press freedom is not enshrined in a written constitution (the UK doesn't have one), it is a 'given' of our culture — something that we pride ourselves on, but perhaps don't examine too closely.

However, there are certain points that need to be taken into consideration here, before it is possible to accept (or reject) this view of the British press as 'free', and decide exactly what we mean when we talk about press freedom. What is news? Who owns the press? Who pays for newspapers? Should newspapers be politically or ideologically impartial?

WHAT IS NEWS?

News is a late Middle English word that means 'tidings, new information of recent events'. Even if we accept this definition as a useful description of what a newspaper delivers, this definition has to be narrowed, as any happening anywhere in the world could be seen as a recent event – SID SMITH EATS CHOCOLATE BAR – EXCLUSIVE. A more useful definition might be 'information about recent events that are of interest to a sufficiently large group, or that may affect the lives of a sufficiently large group'. This definition allows for the difference between local and national newspapers, and for the differences between newspapers of different countries or cultural groups.

However, this definition is still not satisfactory. As was noted above, everything that happens anywhere in the world is a *recent event*, so some-one, somewhere has to decide which, of all the events that have happened over the last 24 hours, are to be included in a specific newspaper, and which are to be excluded. Newspapers can't include everything. These decisions are generally seen as editorial decisions. If an editor excludes an item because he or she thinks that the readership of the newspaper will not be interested in, or do not need, that information, that may be seen as legitimate editorial control. It does mean, though, that these decisions are being made on behalf of the reader. The reader will not be able to comment on that decision, because the reader will probably not be aware that the omitted item of information exists.

The selection of items to put on the news pages may also affect the way in which the reader is presented with the world. For example, a few years ago, newspaper readers were presented with large numbers of stories about attacks by dogs on adults and children. Certain breeds of dog were demonised. Rottweilers became 'devil dogs', and pit bull terriers were given the status of man-eating tigers. This spate of stories may actually have been the prime mover behind changes in legislation that were rather unwisely rushed through Parliament to restrict the ownership and handling of certain breeds. This legislation is now (in 1997) being revised as largely unworkable. Dogs still attack people, and probably always have, but this no longer makes front page stories.

Decisions may be made to exclude information because it is felt necessary to conceal that information from the readership, or to include information that that is seen as in some way beneficial to groups other than

4

the readership – the advertisers, the owners of the paper, the political party the owners of the paper support. Again, the readers have little or no control over what is or is not being presented, as they may not have access to other sources of information against which to judge the content of a newspaper.

People who attend public demonstrations often complain afterwards either that a very well-attended demonstration was ignored by the media and therefore, in the eyes of the majority of the population who did not attend, did not happen, or that it was trivialised by the media's focusing on one aspect – an incident of unruly behaviour, for example, or the dress of a celebrity who attended the event. People who have been involved in newsworthy events that have been ignored or misrepresented by the newspapers often find themselves wondering what else may be excluded from coverage, or presented in a misleading way, but this may not be an issue that the majority of readers are particularly aware of.

DO NEWSPAPERS CONTAIN NEWS?

One reason for this is that newspapers are not read entirely for their informative content. Newspapers contain more than just the news of the day, but even the news is presented in a particular way. We talk about 'news stories'. Other texts that deliver information are not referred to as 'stories'. We don't talk about 'report stories' or 'lecture stories' or 'text-book stories'. A story is an 'account of imaginary or past events, narrative tale, anecdote ... *colloquial* fib'. Why are news stories referred to in a way that gives them the status of fictional accounts? The definition 'account of past events' may to some extent relate to a factual account, but carries the implication of interpretation, elaboration, the creation of a narrative.

Activity

The four following texts are the opening paragraphs of a popular novel, a broadsheet newspaper report, a tabloid newspaper report, an academic paper. Three of the texts (the academic paper and the newspapers) could be seen as texts designed to deliver information; the novel is designed to deliver narrative.

Can you say which text belongs to which genre?

What similarities and differences exist between these texts? You might want to consider overall length of text, sentence length, vocabulary, content, devices used to gain/maintain audience interest.

Text 1: Power Failure

When the power went I was finishing a ten-page report. My office turned black; the computer groaned to a halt. Helpless, I watched the words fade to a ghostly outline that glowed on the screen before vanishing, like the mocking grin of the Cheshire cat.

Text 2: Monarchy Doomed, Say Half of Britons

Six years ago it was unthinkable. Three divorces, an ongoing debate about the royal finances, and one toe-sucking incident later it is reality – more than half of the Queen's subjects believe the royal family is doomed.

Text 3: I had a nail in me 'ead for 22 years!

Dad Robin Hanshaw walked around for 22 years without realising he had a NAIL embedded in his head.

Text 4: A Comparison of Oral and Written Code Elaboration

The Bernstein initiated model of verbal code elaboration and code restriction is well established in sociolinguistic research literature. Studies emanating from England, the United States, and Australia have tended to support the Bernstein thesis of social class differences in language utilisation especially in manipulating the syntactic and semantic components of language which facilitate precision, flexibility and complexity in verbal encoding. Such differences have been noted in both oral and written communication. However, there has been little interest shown to date in comparing elaborated or restricted codes in oral and written language samples for the same subjects, whether of middle or working class origin.

Text 1 is from the novel *Tunnel Vision* by Sara Paretsky. Texts 2 and 3 are from the *Guardian* and the *Sun* respectively, 6 January 1997. Text 4 is from an academic paper: M.E. Poole and T.W. Field, in *Language and Speech*, vol. 19.

The overall length of the texts varies considerably, though they are each the first paragraph of the text from which they have been taken. By far the longest, twice as long as any of the other texts, is the extract from the academic paper. The novel and the broadsheet texts are very close: 46 words and 43 words. The shortest text, from the tabloid article, is 28 words long. The number of sentences is different in each case, but the average sentence length in the novel and the two newspapers is very close — 15, 18 and 18.

The word choices of the texts show a similar pattern. Texts 1, 2 and 3 all use words from everyday vocabulary. There are no words that are from specialist fields, and no words that would send the majority of the population to the dictionary. The longest word in any of these three texts is three syllables long. Text 4, on the other hand, uses a number of specialist words and phrases, 'verbal code elaboration', 'sociolinguistics', and a high number of formal, Latinate words. Several words are as many as five syllables long.

The contents of the first three texts also have some similarities. Each text introduces the reader to a character or characters, and gives some information about events and circumstances. Text 4, on the other hand, is very impersonal, and outlines an area of linguistic theory.

The newspaper texts and the novel all seem constructed to arouse and hold the interest of the reader. Paretsky's novel opens with a subordinate clause 'When the power failed . . .' that immediately arouses the reader's curiosity: what happened?

The *Guardian* opens its article with the sentence 'Six years ago it was unthinkable'. The pronoun 'it' has no reference yet. Again, the reader's curiosity is appealed to: what was unthinkable?

The *Sun* uses a different device to interest readers. It presents them with an incredible fact, a device often used by novelists (for example, Kafka opens his short story 'Metamorphosis' with the line 'As Gregor Samsa awoke one morning from uneasy dreams he found himself transformed in his bed into a gigantic insect'). The first three texts also use a range of language devices to make the texts attractive to the reader. There is use of metaphor in texts 1 and 2 ('turned black', 'a ghostly outline', 'like the mocking grin'; 'doomed'), text 3 uses the speaking voice of its main character, as does text 1. None of these devices is found in text 4.

It isn't just that these texts relate to completely different topics. Text 1 is about computer failure, text 2 about the future of the British monarchy, text 3 about an unusual medical situation and text 4 about the way people use language. Any of these topics could have been approached in a different way. Texts 1, 2 and 3 adopt a similar, narrative stance (people and circumstances) which text 4 does not use. Why is it that newspaper texts appear to be closer to texts whose function it is to tell stories than texts whose function it is to deliver information?

Newspapers, therefore, do contain news, in line with the definition given above, but there is some reason to believe that this news may be presented in the form of a story, rather than as information. This point will be looked at again in Unit 6.

WHO OWNS THE PRESS?

An important factor in the existence of a free press is ownership. The owner of a newspaper has the power to influence the content of the paper, its political stance and its editorial perspective. There has probably never been a time when a newspaper owner did not influence in some way what appeared in that paper. A diverse range and a large number of newspaper owners seems to be an important factor in ensuring that as wide a range of views and interests is represented in the press. The pattern in late twentieth-century Britain has been of newspapers coming into the ownership of smaller numbers of competing groups. In 1965, there were 11 companies owning newspapers, and 19 national titles (including 7 Sunday papers). By 1995, 7 companies owned newspapers, and the number of titles had increased to 21 (including 8 Sunday papers).

This concentration of newspapers in fewer hands, and in the hands of larger, more diverse organisations, clearly has implications for press freedom.

WHO PAYS FOR NEWSPAPERS?

Newspapers in the West exist within a free market system. If they are not successful commercially they will fail. Competition is seen to operate to ensure a high-quality product. If, the argument runs, the newspaper is of a poor quality, then people will not buy it. The free-market operates on one major premise: profit. To this end, newspapers do not only contain news, they also contain comment, advertising, entertainment. Advertising is a vital source of revenue for all newspapers. Sales and circulation figures are also vital to a newspaper's survival. If these figures are low, then advertisers will not want to pay for space in the newspapers. If the readers of a particular newspaper want to be entertained, want information about celebrities and soap-opera characters, and don't want their received ideas challenged, then editors will give them what they want. Mass-circulation newspapers must cater to the requirements of the mass-market, and in this way, the operation of market forces is likely to work against provision for minority interests, or the development of new areas of interest.

Look back to the analysis you did on p. 2. A brief survey of this kind will quickly establish that newspapers do not primarily concern themselves with news, and the news that they do include is fairly circumscribed as to topic area. Broadsheet newspapers contain slightly more news overall than tabloids, and a lot more overseas news, but the bulk of the content in both cases is devoted to other things.

This is not a problem as such, but it does indicate that even newspapers operating within a free market system are not necessarily going to give a free account of the news of the day.

More worrying, though, is the influence of the advertisers and the owners. Newspapers that attract a lot of advertising can sell their product at a lower price and afford a whole range of devices to make their product attractive to the potential reader. If an advertiser has a luxury product, particularly a luxury food product, to sell, does that advertiser want the audience disturbed by reports of poverty and famine? If a major company has been polluting the environment and supporting state terrorism in a developing country, is that company going to give its lucrative advertising contracts to publications that report these events? Is a paper whose editorial policy is to criticise the capitalist and free market system going to attract any advertising at all? As has already been discussed, newspaper owners are often large corporations with a wide range of commercial and political interests. Will such an owner allow stories that are hostile to his/her commercial or political interests to appear in the paper?

The reader of newspapers, then, is not entirely the recipient of *new information on recent events*. He or she is the recipient of selected information on recent events, and this information may well be presented with an ideological 'spin' that makes it very difficult for the reader to make an independent decision on what his/her actual viewpoint of these events actually is.

SHOULD NEWSPAPERS BE IMPARTIAL?

A further important issue relates to the way news is presented. The analysis carried out on pp. 5-6 above demonstrates that newspapers present facts in a way that is designed to arouse the reader's interest and curiosity. It is also possible to present facts in a way that will influence the reader's view of them. This point will be an important focus of this book, but a brief look here at the political bias that appears to exist currently in the press, and the problems presented by press ownership, will give an important context to the problem of the way newspapers present information to their readers.

Before 1970, the political balance of the press was fairly evenly divided between the two main political parties, Conservatives and Labour. Individual newspapers were politically partisan, but the *Daily Herald* and the *Daily Mirror* gave the Labour Party a good share of press support. In the early 1970s, newspapers were not, on the whole, extreme in their partisanship. The *Daily Telegraph*, which was a Conservative-supporting paper, was not particularly hostile to Labour politicians. The *Daily Mirror*, a Labour supporter, was sympathetic to Heath's Conservative government.

After 1975, commercial and political factors led to much greater partisanship in the press, and by the 1979 election, the majority of news-papers supported the Conservative Party, including the *Sun*, which had previously been the *Daily Herald/Sun*, a staunch supporter of Labour. By the 1992 election, one study showed a bias in the press towards the Conservative Party of about 43 percentage points, as against a gap of 8 per cent between the voters (Tunstall, 1996, pp. 240-1). The importance of political bias in the press needs to be looked at in the context of the British electoral system. The 'first past the post' system means that a party can win a massive parliamentary majority on a very small per-centage win over their opponents. Small swings in support can have major consequences for election results. As the *Sun* itself said after the 1992 election: IT'S THE SUN WOT WON IT! However, in the run up to the 1997 election, the *Sun* announced that it was supporting the Labour Party, which subsequently won.

The problem of bias in the press is not a matter of who, or of what system, is supported. The problem is that the bias exists, and the system through which our press operates seems guaranteed to ensure that bias will continue. A mature, healthy democracy needs a system that will allow members of that democracy to decide freely and in an informed manner by what system they want to live. If people are not given the information, it is difficult for them to exercise their choices appropriately.

In the meantime, it is important that readers of newspapers become critical readers, who are aware of, and can identify, gaps and swings in the information they are given. This book is designed to help that process.

Headlines

WHAT IS A HEADLINE?

The headline is a unique type of text. It has a range of functions that specifically dictate its shape, content and structure, and it operates within a range of restrictions that limit the freedom of the writer. For example, the space that the headline will occupy is almost always dictated by the layout of the page, and the size of the typeface will similarly be restricted. The headline will rarely, if ever, be written by the reporter who wrote the news story. It should, in theory, encapsulate the story in a minimum number of words, attract the reader to the story and, if it appears on the front page, attract the reader to the paper.

This mix of functions immediately presents a problem: headlines can often, in their attempt to attract a reader to a story, be ambiguous or confusing. This unit looks at the function of headlines, and the linguistic and graphological devices that headline writers use to create headlines that are effective.

WHAT ARE HEADLINES FOR?

Newspapers are ephemeral texts, that is, they are intended only for the day they are delivering the news. They cater for a wide range of readers with a wide range of needs. Some people may read the paper thoroughly, taking in every aspect; others, probably the majority, skip certain sections and read others in more detail. Some may read only one section. And, of course, each reader may change his/her mode of reading depending on the demands of the day. The headline has the capacity to encapsulate a story, and the headlines in a particular edition give the reader the overall picture of the current news (headline content), its relative importance (visual impact and position in the paper), its classification (which section of the paper it's in - sports, finance, overseas news, etc.). In theory, then, the reader can skim the headlines and have an outline of the news of the day, and some idea of its relative impact and importance. The question is, to what extent do headlines actually work in this way?

Activity

Here is a selection of headlines from a range of newspapers from Tuesday, 30 July 1996. They are in random order, and not classified according to newspaper.

◎ Can you tell, from the headline, what the story is about?
◎ If you were an editor, which of these stories would you put on the front page of your paper?
◎ Which would be your lead (most important) story?

Compare your answers with someone else's. How much agreement is there?

Text: Headlines

1	SHEARER SCORES RECORD £15m FEE
2	CLARKE FACES FURY AS HE RULES OUT TAX CUTS
3	JOIN THE KEW FOR THE BLOOM WITH A PHEW
4	PARENTS' ANGER AS PC IN DEATH CRASH IS CLEARED
5	BURUNDI ARMY KILLS HUTU VILLAGERS IN WAKE OF COUP
6	WOMAN CHIEF CONSTABLE BACKS LEGALISED BROTHELS
7	LONG MAY SHE REIN!
8	THE NURSE FROM HELL

Commentary

These headlines come from seven national newspapers. Story 1, about footballer Alan Shearer's record transfer fee, appeared on the front page of all seven papers, and was the lead story in three.

Story 2, about Kenneth Clarke's refusal to cut taxes, appears in only one paper, as a front page story, but not the lead story.

Story 4, about a police driver who faced a charge of dangerous driving after killing a nurse, appears in all the papers, as a front page story in one, an important inside pages story in four and as a news 'short' in two.

Story 5 appears in three papers, two as a front page story and one as an inside story.

Story 6 appears in all the newspapers, in two cases on the front page, and is the lead story for one of these papers. It appears as an important inside story in the others. The story concerns senior police officers suggesting that licensing brothels may result in a drop in the crime rate. One of these officers was a woman.

Stories 3, 7 and 8 all have headlines that are difficult to understand without the accompanying story. Story 3 refers to the bloom of a tropical plant that was about to open, apparently releasing a powerful and unpleasant smell. Story 7 refers to Camilla Parker Bowles, and the fact that Prince Charles had, apparently, bought her a horse as a present. Story 8 refers to a newly invented robotic nurse. Story 7 appeared in only one paper, but was a front page story. Stories 3 and 8 appeared in all the papers, but on the inside pages.

A quick look across the headlines like this makes it clear that headlines are of limited use in giving a clear overview on the news of the day, or the relative importance of the items. A reader getting all his or her news from newspaper headlines would be forced to assume that the most important event that occurred on 30 July 1996 was the £15 million transfer of a football player.

Did you, as an individual, agree with the importance given to the main stories, and was there agreement within the group? If there were disagreements, what did they revolve around?

THE LANGUAGE OF HEADLINES

This section looks at the language and structure of headlines.

Rapping, slamming, probing and blasting: the vocabulary of the headline writer

Over time, headline writers have developed a vocabulary that fulfils the requirements of the headline, using words that are short, attention-getting and effective. Many of the words that are 'typical' of the headline are probably rarely found outside this particular text type. A few may move from the headline into a wider field.

Activity

Try to find one word to replace the words and phrases in the following list, that would be appropriate to use in a headline.

To reprimand or tell off; to follow someone or to be pursued by someone or something; a person who has behaved dishonourably; excellent or first-class; to defeat soundly; to investigate; political corruption; to increase rapidly; to decrease rapidly; an informer or to inform; to criticise strongly; to make a strong commitment or promise.

Commentary

Words you may have used include rap, dog or stalk, rat, crack (or ace), thrash, probe, sleaze, spiral or soar, slump, grass, slam or blast, vow.

PUTTING WORDS IN: WHAT THE HEADLINE WRITER INCLUDES

The majority of the headline words discussed in the previous section are not chosen just as devices to use space economically. They also have the effect of being attention-getting. The headline writer has a range of linguistic devices available to create headlines that will attract the reader's interest.

Activity

In each of the following groups of headlines, certain words and phrases have been highlighted. Can you suggest why these particular words have been used? What effect is created?

Group 1

1   WOMEN WHO SMOKE HAVE **LIGHTER** CHILDREN
2   DR SPUHLER WILL MAINTAIN **SWISS ROLE**
3   BUTTER BATTLE **SPREADS**
4   MORE WATER MONEY GOES **DOWN THE DRAIN**
5   BIRDS' EGGS GANG **CRACKED**

Group 2

1   **BABE IN WOOD** FOUND SAFE
2   EXPLORER **COMES IN FROM THE COLD**
3   JOIN THE KEW FOR **THE BLOOM WITH A PHEW**

Group 3

1   QUEEN BACKS **DI's DINNER DOWN** UNDER
2   **HIT AND MYTH**
3   **BUTTER BATTLE** SPREADS
4   JOIN THE **KEW** FOR THE BLOOM WITH A **PHEW**

Group 4

1   MAJOR **VOWS** TO OVERRULE GUN TORIES
2   GENIUS REV **BUTCHERED** AT CHURCH
3   EU BOSS FISCHLER **HIT** BY SALMONELLA **SCANDAL**
4   MERGER GROUP **SLAMMED** BY BLUNKETT

Commentary

Headline writers use a range of language devices to make their headlines memorable and striking. These groups each give examples of some of these devices in action.

Word and meaning: Group 1

All the headlines in group 1 play on the potential for ambiguity that can exist in the relationship between word and meaning. For example, the phrase 'Swiss role' is a **homophone** of the phrase 'Swiss roll' (i.e. it is identical in sound). A serious political story is therefore headlined by a linguistic joke. Headline 1, a story about the risks of smoking in pregnancy contains an ambiguous use of the word 'lighter'. This word 'lighter' is a homonym (i.e. it has more than one meaning, and these meanings are not obviously related). It can be an adjective meaning less heavy — the factual meaning required by the story, but it can also be a noun meaning a device for lighting (in this case) a cigarette. Headline 3 makes use of the fact that the word 'spreads' is a **polyseme** (i.e. it has several closely related meanings). Butter can be spread, battles can widen. Headlines 4 and 5 make use of metaphorical associations. 'To go down the drain' is what water literally does, but this phrase is also widely used to mean wasted (all that effort just went down the drain); 'cracked' is a word that is popular with headline users, and is a slang term for solved, but of course eggs literally crack — hence the headline.

Intertextuality: Group 2

Any culture will have a range of familiar phrases and sayings, and in the case of our particular culture, many of these come from popular songs, book titles, etc. Headline writers often make reference to these, as in the examples in group 2. For example, Headline 1 refers to a well-known folk tale, 'The Babes in the Wood'. Headlines 2 and 3 make reference to the titles of well-known novels: John le Carré's *The Spy Who Came in From the Cold*, and E.M. Forster's *A Room With a View*.

Phonology: Group 3

Though headlines are written to be read, not spoken, a very common way of making headlines memorable is to use the reader's awareness of sound. Headlines 1 and 3 use alliteration on /d/ and /b/, and headline 2 uses the phonological similarity between 'myth' and 'miss' to make reference to the phrase hit and miss. Headline 4 uses rhyme — 'Kew' and 'phew', and also uses a homophone to make a pun on 'Kew', the place where the event is taking place, and the 'queue' that will form to see this flower with the unpleasant smell.

Loaded words: Group 4

In order to make headlines attract the attention of the reader, headline writers may select words that carry particularly strong **connotations**, that is, carry an emotional loading beyond their literal meaning. A good example in the data is the word 'butchered' in headline 2. This word has the dictionary meaning of 'to slaughter and cut up an animal'. When it is applied to a human being, it carries both the meaning of extreme and cruel violence, and also implies that the killer must have seen the victim as having the same status as an animal.

TAKING WORDS OUT: WHAT THE HEADLINE WRITER OMITS

Activity

Look at the following headlines, and rewrite them in clear standard English, by adding any missing words. Try not to make any other changes.

1   MURDER MYSTERY OF ROBBED MOTHER
2   RUNCIE TURNS ON ROYALS AS WRITER DEFENDS REVELATIONS
3   CYCLE BOOM GOES FLAT
4   TOBACCONISTS FUMING
5   MINISTRY TO HOLD TALKS ON REVIEW
6   COUNCILLORS TO ACT ON STRIP SHOWS

What classes of words are headline writers likely to omit, and why?

Commentary

The words you might have added to the headlines include 'the', 'a', 'are', 'were', 'is' and often titles such as 'Mr', 'Sir', 'Archbishop', etc. The headline writer needs to include the factual detail of the story in a way that will attract the reader's attention. Given that space is limited, **lexical words** (words that have meaning, such as nouns, main verbs, adjectives, adverbs) are far more useful to the writer than **grammatical words** (words that signal grammatical relationships, such as determiners − 'the', 'a', 'this', 'that', etc., auxiliary verbs 'be', 'have', 'do'). But this can occasionally lead to ambiguity, as many lexical words depend on grammatical words to establish which word class they are. This can lead to headlines such as:

1   MINE EXPLODED
2   8TH ARMY PUSH BOTTLES UP GERMANS
3   LABOUR PARTY SPLIT LOOMS
4   POLICE FIND CONSTABLE DRAWING IN ATTIC

The reader is left floundering as the meaning is almost irretrievably ambiguous until the accompanying article is read. 'Mine' actually refers to an explosive weapon, but in this context looks much more like a possessive pronoun ('Mine exploded.' 'That's funny. Mine didn't.').

The second headline is an often-quoted WW2 headline. The words 'push' and 'bottles' are used with their less usual meanings. 'Push' in this

19

case is a noun, meaning 'advance'. 'Bottles' is part of a **phrasal verb** 'bottles up' meaning 'block' or 'trap'. (Phrasal verbs are verbs that consist of a verb and a preposition that need to be understood together, for example 'run up' in sentences such as 'The tailor ran up a pair of trousers', 'Mary ran up some steep bills' as opposed to 'The ferret ran up a pair of trousers', 'Mary ran up some steep hills'.) The meaning of the headline is, therefore, '8th army advance traps Germans'.

In the third headline, the ambiguity is caused because there is no way of telling whether 'split' and 'looms' are used as nouns or verbs.

In the fourth, 'Constable drawing' is a noun phrase – a drawing by Constable. In the headline, it looks more like a noun followed by a verb, particularly as the initial word 'police' puts that meaning of 'Constable' in the reader's mind.

SHAKING IT ALL ABOUT: HOW THE HEADLINE WRITER REORGANISES LANGUAGE

In order to produce punchy, economical texts, the headline writer also plays about with the standard order of words and phrases.

Activity

Look at the following headlines. Try to rewrite the highlighted sections in clear standard English. (Headline 1 refers to a pensioner who wrote to a Tory minister criticising the recent pay rise that MPs had awarded themselves.)

1   MPS FURY AT **PAY RAP OAP**
2   **'BANDIT' CAR CHASE POLICE INSTRUCTOR** FINED $750 AFTER DEATH OF NURSE
3   **HANDOUTS PROBE**
4   GRID CHIEF BLASTS **'£5 OFF BILLS' CALL**

The highlighted sections are all **noun phrases**.

Nouns form patterns with other words to form noun phrases. A noun phrase will always contain a noun. The shortest possible noun phrase consists of a single noun, e.g. 'cars', 'people'. The main noun in a noun phrase is called the **headword**. Noun phrases can also contain determiners – 'the', 'a', 'these', etc., producing a two-word noun phrase: 'these cars', 'the people', 'a pensioner'. More information can be included in the noun phrase by adding a **modifier** between the determiner and the noun: 'these fast cars', 'the important people', 'an angry pensioner'. Noun phrases can have more than one modifier, 'these fast sports cars', 'the important political people', 'the angry Yorkshire pensioners'. Modifiers can add various kinds of information about a noun, including descriptive detail – 'blue sky', 'the sweet perfume', 'a misty morning'; number – 'the three people'; kind or type – 'Yorkshire pensioners'.

Headline writers often put information into the modifier slot in the noun phrase, to produce a form of shorthand that is a very distinctive feature of newspaper style. For example, the story covered by headline 2 is about a police driving instructor involved in a fatal car crash when he was chasing another car as part of a training exercise. This fairly complex piece of information is encapsulated in a long noun phrase. The phrase 'police instructor' gives information about the person responsible for the accident. The phrase 'car chase', used to modify police instructor, gives the event, and the word 'bandit', graphologically marked with inverted commas to indicate that this was not a real police chase, gives the context in which the event took place.

Many words have the capacity to **class-shift**, that is, to operate as more than one word class. For example, 'chase' can be either a noun or a verb, 'a chase' or 'to chase'. By using chase as a noun in headline 2, the writer manages to include the action – chase – without having to include it as a verb. Some headlines omit the verb completely by implying the action within the noun phrase. The capacity the noun phrase has for modification makes this particular structure a very flexible one, and therefore extremely useful to the headline writer.

Activity

Here are three news stories, outlined briefly in standard English. Turn the second and third into single noun phrases that would make appropriate headlines, and then label the modifiers and the headword for each noun phrase. The first one has been done as an example.

◎ A Labrador, Daisy, has had to have emergency veterinary treatment after she ate a daffodil.
◎ A man who killed two pensioners when he attempted to steal their money has escaped from custody.
◎ The local police are investigating a teacher's house as they believe she has been running a brothel on the premises.

21

A possible headline for the first story would be: DAFFY DAISY'S VET-DASH PANIC

mod	*mod*	*mod*	*headword*
DAFFY	DAISY'S	VET-DASH	PANIC

Activity

You now have a list of devices that are used by headline writers to create effective headlines.

- ◎ Word choice
- ◎ Word play
- ◎ Intertextuality
- ◎ Sound
- ◎ Loaded language
- ◎ Omission of grammatical words
- ◎ Noun phrases
- ◎ Class shift

Using one or more of the following texts for the factual details of your story, write three headlines. Try to use each device at least once.

Text 1

> Hey diddle diddle, the cat and the fiddle
> The cow jumped over the moon
> The little dog laughed to see such fun
> And the dish ran away with the spoon

Text 2

> Tom-Tom the piper's son
> Stole a pig and away did run
> The pig was eat
> Tom was beat
> Tom went roaring down the street

Text 3

There was a young man of high rank
Who went to sea in a tank
They said 'It is sad,
He surely is mad!'
And he proved they were right when he sank.

Text 4

There was a young man from Japan
Whose poetry never would scan
When they asked him why
He said with a sigh,
'It's because I put as many words into the last line as I possibly can.'

Swap your headlines with another group. Can they link your headlines with the correct story?

GRAPHOLOGICAL FEATURES OF HEADLINES

Headlines also have a visual function. The print is larger than the text of the main articles they refer to, but front page headlines, particularly in tabloid newspapers, can by themselves occupy more space than the whole article they refer to.

Headlines work in conjunction with the other visual aspects of the newspaper text, in particular the pictures. A story about a plane crash used the headline AND THEY ALL LIVED. This only carries meaning because it was accompanied by a picture of the crashed plane. The example below operates in a similar way, except that the headline is not completely obscure without the picture - but the picture adds an extra dimension of meaning!

23

Text: Diana

Diana's fingers do the talking

New beginning: Diana, Princess of Wales leaves an English National Ballet lunch appointment yesterday

HEADLINES AS INFORMATION

The conflicting roles of the headline – to carry information and to attract the attention of the reader – were discussed briefly above (p. 13). This section looks at the way the headline delivers information, and what, from the point of view of the headline writer, the information actually is in relation to the story.

If a relatively simple definition of information is used, the headline should deliver some detail on what happened, who was involved, where it happened, what the circumstances were. This can be simplified into **what, who, where, how**. Most models of information would include a when and a why element, but as daily newspapers tend to deal with the immediate events, the when can generally be understood. The why tends to be addressed in the article rather than the headline. To what extent, then, do headlines perform this what-where-who-how function?

The following headlines all appeared on 14 August 1996, and relate to the same story. Take each headline individually and decide

◎   What information does each headline give you?
◎   What are the most important areas of information as far as this headline writer is concerned?

1   LUCKY ESCAPE AS PLANE SKIDS ONTO MOTORWAY
2   AND THEY ALL LIVED
3   ACTRESS LISA'S AMAZING JET CRASH ESCAPE
4   FOUR GOT OUT OF THIS ALIVE
5   CLEESE'S FILM PAL IN PLANE CRASH ESCAPE
6   CLEESE GIRL JET MIRACLE

Analysing headline language from a **what, who, where, how** model (the **wh-model**) presents immediate difficulties, because the headline is not necessarily an independent text, and also the structure of the language may be non-standard. Identifying **who** is not difficult, but **what** can be more of a problem. In most contexts, this would be represented by a verb. Headlines may not contain a verb. The action is frequently nominalised (turned into a noun), which can distance the word or phrase from the actual action. It may be useful here to try to draw from the headlines some factual information and reconstruct the story, which is as follows:

A plane crashed onto a motorway. Four people were on board. Luckily, no one died.

The information from the headlines above can now be shown like this:

Actors / participants	Action	Location of action	Other
			circumstances / comment
plane	skids, (escape)	onto motorway	lucky escape
they all	lived		
actress Lisa	(escape), (crash)		amazing jet crash escape
four	got out	this	alive
Cleese's film			
pal	(escape), (crash)		plane crash escape
Cleese girl			jet miracle

Note: The bracketed words make reference to actions, but are not verbs in the headlines.

How do these headlines work as carriers of information from the wh-model? Headline 1 uses the inanimate 'plane', and allows the reader to make the assumption, to presuppose, that there were passengers and crew aboard.

Headlines 2 and 4 use **deictic reference**, that is reference that depends on the context for its meaning. Deictic language can be defined as language that points, that requires either shared knowledge or an external reference. 'Meet me here at this time tomorrow' only works if addresser and addressee know where 'here' is, and what time 'this time' is. Similarly, a note on a door saying 'back in 10 minutes' means nothing to the reader unless he or she knows what time it was when the writer left. Reference of this kind is deictic. The examples here, headlines 2 and 4, require a photograph to give meaning to the words **they, this,** and **four.**

Headlines 3, 5 and 6 give the reader specific but incomplete or misleading information. 'Lisa', 'Cleese's film pal' and 'Cleese girl' give information about one participant. However, another participant emerges in two of these headlines, actor and writer John Cleese. From an information point of view, this is wasted space, because John Cleese was not involved in any way in this incident. The information that 'Lisa' is an actress could also be seen as secondary to the facts of the event. These headlines direct the reader away from the event and towards the area of media celebrity.

These headlines are, therefore, not very efficient in giving the reader **who** information.

If **what** in the model is considered as the verb element, **what happened**, similar devices are used. Headline 1 uses direct reference to action: skids. In all the other headlines, the reference is indirect. It will be useful here to look at the structure of the phrases used to represent the action in headlines 3, 5 and 6.

In each case, the event of the crash is nominalised, that is, turned into a noun. Instead of using a structure such as PLANE CRASHES, these headline writers have chosen to use noun phrases: 'amazing jet crash escape', 'plane crash escape', 'jet miracle'. Headline 6 removes the idea of a crash altogether, and in headlines 3 and 5, the headword, the main focus of the noun phrase, is the word 'escape'. The word 'crash' is used in a position of less focus, as a modifier in the noun phrase.

In headlines 2 and 4, the reference to the crash is deictic, that is, dependent on the context. The action relates to the event of survival: 'lived' and 'got out'.

The **what** element is, therefore, focused very much on the fact that people survived this particular accident, rather than on the fact that the accident itself happened.

If **how** is taken to cover circumstance, then the headlines also deal with this. It is unusual for there to be any survivors of a plane crash, and this is the circumstance that the headline writers focus on, directly in the case of headlines 1, 3 and 6 that use the words 'lucky', 'amazing' and 'miracle'; and by linking with the graphology in headlines 2 and 4. Headline 5 confines itself to the use of the word 'escape', which, combined with 'jet crash', implies a lucky escape.

The where and when elements are largely ignored. Headline 1 gives the information that the plane crashed onto a motorway, the other headlines ignore this.

There is, therefore, very little consensus about the 'facts' surrounding this news story. All the papers agree on the importance of the 'luck' element, but only three of them inform the reader of the fact that no one was killed. The other three only give this information about one passenger. Headline 1 gives 'luck' information, the fact that the plane skidded, and the information about the motorway. Headlines 2 and concentrate on the luck element alone. Headline 3 focuses on one passenger, an actress, and headlines 5 and 6 concentrate on actor and writer John Cleese, who was not actually involved in the event.

HEADLINES AS OPINION MANIPULATORS

Headlines have a persuasive function when they are designed to attract the attention of the reader and interest him/her in reading the story (or in the case of front page headlines, in buying the newspaper), but they can also be written to influence the opinion of the reader. This next section considers headlines that appeared the day the divorce of the Prince and Princess of Wales became absolute.

This is an interesting story from a newspaper point of view, not just for its royal content which always excites the tabloids, but because it was not, in one sense, news at all. The information that the divorce would become absolute on 29 August 1996 was widely known. What the story did give the papers was the chance to rehash the 'royal soap' that the story completed. Effectively, newspaper readers were asked to take sides.

(Sun)

1   BYE BYE BIG EARS
2   I'LL ALWAYS WEAR HIS RING
3   THAT'S MADE MY DI
4   I FELT LUMP IN MY THROAT AS I LIFTED CAMERA
5   GOD SAVE WONDERFUL DI
6   YOU WILL LOVE AGAIN
7   YOU'LL ALWAYS BE THE QUEEN OF HEARTS

(Daily Mail)

8   DIVORCED: BUT STILL SHE WEARS HIS RING
9   TWO £10 NOTES AND THE DREAM IS OVER
10 ICE COOL IN ICE BLUE . . . ANXIOUS IN AN ANORAK

(Mirror)

11 DIANA: I'LL RUN RINGS ROUND CHARLES
12 PM: ROYALTY WILL SURVIVE
13 WITH THIS RING I THEE SHED
14 NEW RULES OVER HRH

15   NO TEARS, NO TREMBLING LIP

16   PRAYERS FOR DI AT ST PAULS

(Telegraph)

17   DIANA'S FINGERS DO THE TALKING

How do these headlines represent the protagonists in this story, and to what extent are the constitutional implications of this story addressed?

Activity

For each of the newspapers quoted, list the names or pronouns used to refer to:

> The Prince of Wales
> The Princess of Wales
> The Queen
> Other

What attitudes does the naming suggest to each of the protagonists involved?

Commentary

The *Sun* makes two references to the Prince of Wales, 'big ears' and 'his'. The Princess of Wales is named or referred to six times, 'I', 'Di', 'Di', 'you', 'you', 'queen of hearts'.

The *Daily Mail* makes only one direct reference to each, 'she' and 'his'.

The *Mirror* makes four references to the Princess, 'Diana', 'I', 'I', 'Di'; and two to the Prince, 'Charles', 'thee'.

The *Telegraph* only makes reference to the Princess, 'Diana's'.

The other protagonists in the affair are barely mentioned in the headlines. There is an apparent reference to the Queen in the *Sun* 'my', and the *Mirror* refers to the Prime Minister, 'PM', but the wider constitutional implications of the divorce of the heir to the throne are not addressed in the headlines. The *Sun* involves itself in the story by headlining a quote from a photographer 'I'.

The focus of the stories is, therefore, clearly on the Princess. The references to her are sympathetic 'queen of hearts', friendly (the use of a press-developed nickname) or neutral. The references to the Prince of Wales, on the other hand, are either neutral or hostile 'big ears'. In both the *Sun* (apart from the naming 'big ears') and the *Daily Mail*, reference to the Prince is confined to the possessive determiner 'his'. There are two further references in the *Daily Mail* that do not directly name either the Prince or the Princess, but operate by using pictures to give the reference. In these, the Princess is 'ice cool' in 'ice blue', the Prince is 'anxious' in 'an anorak'. This is an interesting use of connotation: the Princess achieves the desirable quality of cool, the Prince becomes an anorak – a current term of derision.

Activity

The naming devices used in the headlines suggest bias in favour of the Princess. Can you identify other language devices that have this effect? Does the headline represent the spoken voice? Who is 'speaking'? Who is addressed by the headline? How are the protagonists described or represented?

Commentary

In the *Sun* and the *Mirror*, the 'voice' of the princess is apparently heard. The *Sun* gives the reader the pathos of 'I'll always wear his ring', the word 'always' implying fidelity which the reader may want to contrast with the behaviour of the Prince. 'That's made my Di' is accompanied by the photograph of a woman who impersonates the Queen – a queen 'lookalike' (another headline word). This apparent quote from the Queen implies that the royal establishment oppose the Princess. The note of triumph in 'That's made my Di' contrasts clearly with the 'voice' of the Princess. It is a matter of question as to who is saying 'Bye bye big ears'. This could be the 'voice' of the Princess, or it could be the voice of the paper expressing the sentiment it wants its readers to share.

This effect is enhanced by the use of headlines that may be intended to be the 'voice' of the *Sun* readers: 'You will love again', 'You'll always be the queen of hearts'; and, interestingly, a headline that sings the national anthem to someone who is not the sovereign: 'God save wonderful Di'.

The *Mirror*, too, gives the reader the 'voice' of the Princess. This voice is less one of pathos than of revenge: 'I'll run rings round Charles'.

This Princess is not the heartbroken woman of the *Sun*, but someone who is glad to be out of a marriage: 'With this ring, I thee shed'. However, the Princess as victim is not completely absent from this portrayal. The victim is represented by 'tears' and 'trembling lip'; the brave victim by the use of negation: 'No tears, No trembling lip'.

The headlines give the story from a range of apparently different perspectives. There is the 'voice' of the Princess, the 'voice' of the reader, the 'voice' of the newspaper, the 'voice' of the Queen (even though an impersonator is used, the implication is made that this is the Queen's view). It is easy for the reader to forget, or to fail to recognise, that the actual perspective is that of the newspaper. Similarly, the person or people addressed are assumed to share the perspective that the paper offers – that of sympathy for the Princess and hostility towards the Prince. The reader may not, in fact, share this perspective. The paper therefore creates another participant in the story – an **implied reader** to whom the text is addressed.

Actual voice		Implied voice	Actual recipient	Implied recipient
(2)	paper	Princess	reader	implied reader
(5,6,7)	paper	implied reader/paper	reader	Princess
(1,11,13)	paper	Princess	reader	Prince
(1)	paper	paper	reader	Prince
(3)	paper	'Queen'	reader	Princess

The headlines also exclude, or reduce the importance of other perspectives, by the way the headlines are structured. The absence of the Prince from many of the headlines leads to a one-sided picture, but where he is present, the structure of the headline places him in a secondary role, as either the object or adverbial of a verb, whereas the Princess is frequently the subject of the same verb.

Subject	Verb	Direct object	Adverbial
I	'll wear	his ring	always
she	wears	his ring	still
I	'll run rings		round Charles
I	shed	thee	

Note: The headline BYE BYE BIG EARS is similar in that the Prince appears as the vocative object of the salutation BYE BYE.

The overall effect in the tabloid headlines is to present the reader with one point of view to the exclusion of any other. The Princess is the focus of attention, the Princess has the support of the people and the Prince is either unimportant or an object of ridicule.

The *Telegraph*, which might have been expected to present a more serious analysis of the constitutional implications of this affair, sums the whole event up with a combination of picture and headline that gives the reader a clear visual message, and a reference to an advertising slogan for the *Yellow Pages* – 'Let your fingers do the walking' (p. 24).

Summary

Headlines are important in their own right. They are the first text that a newspaper reader sees when buying and reading the paper. They employ a range of creative language devices to produce short, attention-getting, highly memorable texts, and have the capacity to encapsulate an entire story in a few words.

This Unit has looked at some of the devices the headline writer uses to create effective headlines – sound via alliteration, homophones and rhyme; word and meaning via naming, loaded language, ambiguity and word play; syntax via the use of structures designed to focus on specific aspects of the text; non-standard structures, omission of words to create a telegraphic style. Headline writers also use selection of information; and direct and indirect address to readers or other participants in the story.

Lastly, but as importantly, headlines use graphology, the visual aspect of text, to draw the reader's eye. If you, as the reader are visually attracted to a text, and then enticed by an ambiguous or startling text, the newspaper has

GOTCHA

1   Collect and analyse the front page headlines of several newspapers: broadsheet, tabloid and local. Are there any differences between individual newspapers or between types of newspaper?

2   Collect examples of headlines from newspapers of 30 years ago. (Your local library should have back copies of the *Times* on microfilm.) Have headlines changed in the last 30 years? Look at earlier newspapers as well.

3   These headlines appeared in American newspapers (*USA Today*, *International Herald Tribune*, *San Bernadino County Sun*). Do these headlines use similar devices to those used in the British press?

> ISRAEL BLAMES ARAFAT FOR BOMBING
> THE NOMADIC LIFE DRIES UP IN ARABIA
> BUSH REPLICATES '44 PARACHUTE JUMP
> MURDERER'S ATTORNEY DENIES HE ACTED
> INCOMPETENTLY
> SLAYER'S CONVICTION COULD BE REVERSED

Audience

The audience for a newspaper is its reader. This may seem to be too obvious to state, but it raises some important points about the way papers relate to their audience, and the difference between the 'real' audience, the readership, and the audience the paper appears to be writing for – the 'implied' audience. This unit looks at the way newspapers assume the existence of groups that may not actually exist as groups within society and, by addressing themselves to these groups, create a shared ideology that can frequently work to obscure issues rather than clarify them.

WHO READS THE PAPERS?

Newspaper groups do market research and are well aware of the profile of their readership. There are certain assumptions that people tend to make about newspaper readerships: *Sun* readers are supposed to be Tory supporters, and working-class; *Guardian* readers are expected to be left-wing, middle-class, Labour supporters; *Sun* readers are supposed to be younger, *Telegraph* readers older, but these labels are not really very useful or even very accurate.

Surveys done in 1995 show that the *Daily Telegraph* and the *Daily Express* had fewer younger readers (aged 15–44 years) than the *Guardian* and the *Daily Star*. The *Daily Telegraph*, the *Times*, the *Independent* and the

Guardian had a high percentage (over 70 per cent) of middle class – ABC1 – readers, the *Daily Express* and the *Daily Mail* had over 60 per cent ABC1 readers, and the *Daily Mirror*, the *Sun* and the *Daily Star* had over 20 per cent ABC1 readers. At this time, 65 per cent of the readers of both the *Guardian* and the *Daily Star* were aged between 15 and 44 years (Tunstall, 1996, p. 93).

In 1995, a survey showed that 61 per cent of the readership of the *Sun* expressed a preference for Labour (ibid., p. 242).

Activity

Do a quick survey around (1) your group, and (2) your college. Find out who reads what paper, and see if you can identify patterns of readership for particular papers according to age, gender, political sympathies, social class, age.

Commentary

It is unlikely that you are able to profile, from such a survey, a 'typical' *Sun* reader, or a 'typical' *Times* reader. Newspaper readerships tend to be diverse, and you would need to look at large numbers to find any very significant patterns.

HOW NEWSPAPERS IDENTIFY THEIR AUDIENCE

There may be no clear profile of a '*Sun* reader' or a '*Guardian* reader', but the papers themselves often write as though such a person exists and that there is, in fact, a homogeneous group of people with shared beliefs and values whose defining feature is the newspaper that they read.

In the article 'Hula Meanie', '*Sun* readers' are explicitly identified as a group. The article reports that they voted 5–1 in favour of a particular outcome (who is entitled to a prize). The person against whom the '*Sun* readers' voted is a 'meanie', and 'defiant'. Under his photograph he is quoted as saying 'it's not fair'. He 'spurns' and 'snubbed' *Sun* readers.

There are several contexts here. The language of a child's experience is used – 'meanie', 'It's not fair'. These terms are applied to the 'opponent' of the readers. The implication is that his behaviour is childish, and therefore possibly unreasonable. The use of the terms 'spurn' and 'snubbed' imply disdain, contempt and rebuff. The prize money is described as 'loot' – with the implication of ill-gotten gains.

Text: Hula Meanie

HULA MEANIE SPURNS SUN READERS ON LOOT

DEFIANT Steve Maxwell last night snubbed Sun readers by refusing to give a £10,000 Hula Hoops prize to the boy who found it.

Meanie Steve claimed: "I'm being made to look the bad guy and it's just not fair." He has offered £1,800 to 11-year-old Christopher Wright.

But in a weekend You the Jury poll Sun readers voted 5–1 that Christopher and his family should get all the loot.

Christopher found the winning "Twister" Hula Hoop in a 24p packet Steve's wife Jackie gave him. He said Jackie promised him £5,000.

Now parents Gordon and Bernadette are taking legal action.

But Steve, 37, of Wyken, West Midlands,

EXCLUSIVE by ANDREW PARKER

said: "It will take a court to make me hand over £5,000.

"Jackie bought the Hula Hoops and they were her property."

And mum-of-four Jackie added: "Bernadette was a friend of mine but not anymore."

Steve . . . "it's not fair"

The person who opposes the '*Sun* readers' is, therefore, by implication, childish, unreasonable, ill-mannered and dishonest. *Sun* readers are, also by implication, against these qualities, and for maturity, fair play, courtesy and honesty.

The '*Sun* readers', however, are not clearly defined. Who exactly voted 5–1 for a particular outcome? Six people? Six hundred people? Six thousand people? This information is not given.

Activity

Look at the extract from the *Daily Mirror*, and answer the questions that follow.

◎ How does the article identify its audience?
◎ What qualities does this audience have?
◎ What qualities do the people who 'oppose' the audience have?
◎ What actions does each group perform?
◎ What role does the newspaper itself play?

Text: Queen

QUEEN SNUBS 102,625

DAILY Mirror

READERS

THE Queen has delivered an amazing snub to the Daily Mirror's loyal army of readers.

By LUCY TURNER

Buckingham Palace officials refused to accept our massive petition to win back Princess Diana's HRH status.

An astonishing 102,625 readers have now signed up to our campaign urging the Queen to restore the title.

But when we tried to hand over the letters at the palace gates, we were turned away.

The Mirror arrived in style in a horse-drawn carriage, complete with coachman and footman in full regalia.

Arrest

Inside were three bulging sackfuls of letters.

When we drew up, we were threatened with arrest. Then a stony-faced police officer at the gates told us: "Sorry, we were expecting you a couple of days ago with this and I have been told not to take anything from you."

He even refused to accept a personal letter to the Queen urging her to reconsider her decision to strip the princess of her royal title.

"You will have to post it," the officer said.

"We cannot accept it unless it is by courier or by post."

The Mirror made its first-class delivery after an earlier snub from the palace. Last week we handed in about 200 letters summing up the many thousands we have received. But they were rudely returned in a scruffy brown envelope with no covering letter.

Diana lost her HRH status in her recent divorce settlement with Prince Charles.

Commentary

The audience is identified in relation to the newspaper read: '*Mirror* readers'. They are identified as 'the *Daily Mirror*'s loyal army of readers'. The metaphoric reference to the readers as an army adds emphasis to the quality of loyalty, but the image is confusing. Are they the Queen's loyal army – in which case her 'snub' becomes particularly bad – or are they the newspaper's loyal army – in which case they are fighting for justice for the Princess of Wales. The role and identity of the readers becomes more confused as it is engulfed in the identity of the newspaper itself. First there is reference to '*our* massive petition', and '*our* campaign', which moves to '*we* tried to hand over the letters'. At this point it is not entirely clear whether 'our' and 'we' represents the editorial stance of the paper alone, or the paper and its readership. Finally, the paper is personified as 'The Mirror arrived in style'. At this point, the paper itself has become a protagonist in the event, rather than a mechanism for reporting it.

The Queen is the opponent in the *Mirror* story. She 'snubs' the readers, and 'delivers an amazing snub'.

The audience for this article is apparently a group who have signed a petition to the Queen and who feel strongly that Princess Diana should retain the title HRH (Her Royal Highness). This group has made an appeal that has been abruptly and rudely rejected. By identifying this audience as '*Mirror* readers', the paper has included all the readers of that article within the group – though many of them may not share the view about the Princess of Wales, and the majority will probably not have signed the petition.

An interesting aspect of this kind of reporting is that a conflict is established between groups and individuals who have never met, or encountered each other in any way. The 'opponents' of the readers have their actions described in ways that imply their hostility towards these non-existent groups. The descriptions of these opponents are generally negative, either through direct description, or through the words used for their actions.

These stories may not relate to fundamentally important issues – particularly the story about the prize money, which amounts to manufactured news. The *Sun* created a poll, and then reported the results. The *Mirror* too has manufactured a story. The news item is clearly one of legitimate national interest – the future status of the Princess of Wales – but this particular item is, again, a paper placing itself within a story where from a news point of view it really has no role.

This kind of audience creation is overt. The paper identifies the group, names it and champions its cause. The reader of the paper,

39

particularly if he/she is a regular reader, becomes part of that group, and may feel that he/she has been 'snubbed' or in some way insulted or ignored. This can help to promote a sense of group homogeneity that does not, in fact, exist.

THE IDENTITY OF THE READER

It is important to distinguish between the reader as an individual who may or may not read that particular newspaper regularly, and the 'created' reader who is being identified in the text. For the purposes of analysis, the reader as individual will be referred to as **the reader**, the created reader will be referred to as **the implied reader**.

Creating a system of shared values

In the examples discussed in the previous section, the appeal to the implied readership is overt. The group is actually named in the story. A more common way in which papers may identify and address their implied readership is by reporting stories in a way that is designed to evoke one particular response, thus establishing a set of shared values, usually in opposition to another group who do not share, or who attack these values.

One obvious area in which newspapers tend to polarise, and thus try to create different sets of shared values, is in the area of party politics (see the discussion of the role of newspapers in the 1992 election in the introduction p. 10) but it is often more revealing to look at attitudes expressed towards other aspects of our culture - for example gender, ethnicity, family, sexual orientation. It has already been suggested in the previous section that newspaper readers as a group do not exist and do not have the uniformity of views on any given range of topics that some news reporting may suggest. How, then, do newspapers create their implied readership and appeal to this sense of shared values that the implied reader-ship is supposed to have? The next section will address this issue.

THE ROLE OF THE AUDIENCE

If there is no such individual as the '*Sun* reader' or the '*Guardian* reader', why is audience an important concept when the language of newspapers is under consideration?

Language always occurs within a context, and as social users of language individuals know how to respond to linguistic triggers relating to the context of the language situation, the intended message, the feedback and input from others. It could be argued that language is the key factor in the establishment and maintenance of social groups, of society as an entity. Language allows individuals to communicate, to interpret the world and themselves, to express logic, causes and outcomes, to establish relationships within the group. Recent studies into the development of language within the individual suggest that the development of the social skills of language is as crucial as the development of the structural aspects of language. Disorders that affect the development of what are referred to as **pragmatic** skills (as found, for example, in many autistic people) are as disabling as disorders that affect the development at a structural level.

Activity

Look at the following transcripts of language that took place in a variety of contexts. At first glance, these utterances look strange – responses seem irrelevant, statements over-obvious, but all of these exchanges worked, in that all participants understood the intended meaning of the utterance. Can you account for this?

(*Two students*)
A: Are you going to Davo's tonight?
B: It's Thursday.

(*Group of students in a joke-telling session*)
A: How many surrealists does it take to paint a house?
B: Fish.

(*Lecturer and student*)
L: There's a problem with this video.
S: It works better if you plug it in.

(*Student to student*)
A: Where's the pen?
B: Where's your glasses?

Commentary

As individuals and as members of groups, we assume that language contains meaning, and we conduct exchanges with that assumption as an important factor. We tend to look for meaning where it may initially appear to be missing. One possible reason why proof-reading a piece of written text is so difficult is that the reader tends to see what he/she expects to be there rather than what is.

41

Each of these exchanges appears initially to break the rules of meaning. In the first two exchanges, the response seems to be irrelevant. The third one seems to be a classic case of stating the obvious and the fourth one again seems irrelevant because instead of answering the question the second participant responds with another question. However, most people have no problems in sorting these exchanges out.

In the first exchange, it is clear that both parties are aware of some event that happens on Thursdays (or on that particular Thursday) that makes the proposed visit impossible. As they are both aware of this, there is no need to clarify the situation beyond the reminder that is issued − it's Thursday. Any further information would be irrelevant. The second exchange is a joke that plays on the fact that we expect meaning in language. Surrealists by definition operate beyond the expected parameters of meaning, so a totally irrelevant answer completes the joke, which is one of a series of jokes that operates to the same question/answer structure. The third exchange apparently offers unnecessary information, but is, in fact, carrying an implication. The information offered is that a particular piece of equipment isn't plugged in, but a further comment is contained in the way the remark is phrased − the addressee has made a foolish mistake. The fourth exchange operates in a similar way. The reply, apparently irrelevant, carries the information that the addresser hasn't looked closely enough.

There are a whole range of contextual triggers that allow a range of messages to be carried in discourse. These messages, as noted above, help to maintain social role and cohesion. Newspapers function within a social context, and operate, of necessity, within the language framework. By using the social aspects of language, newspapers begin to establish a group identity within the readership.

Activity

Text: Poem fury is part of an article that appeared in the *Daily Mail*, and refers to a planned broadcast of Tony Harrison's poem, 'V'. How does this text place an implied reader within a context that suggests a system of shared values?

- ◎ What emotional context are the writers trying to establish? What emotion do they require of their readers? How does the text achieve this?
- ◎ Who is opposing the broadcast, and how does the text indicate this?
- ◎ What, do you assume, is the subject matter of the poem? What leads you to this assumption?

42

FOUR-LETTER TV POEM FURY

By JOHN DEANS and GARRY JENKINS

BROADCASTERS are lining up for a head-on clash with the political establishment over a planned Channel 4 programme featuring a
5 **torrent of fourletter filth.**

Outraged MPs last night demanded an immediate ban on the screening, which will unleash the most explicitly sexual language yet beamed into the nation's living rooms.

10 And the pressure will be on Home Secretary Douglas Hurd, who is proposing to set up a new watchdog Broadcasting Standards Council, to crack down on the media bosses now.

The cascade of expletives will pour out to viewers at the rate of
15 two a minute during the 45-minute show on November 4. The crudest, most offensive word is used 17 times.

The programme, a filmed recital of a poem called 'V.' written and read by Newcastle
20 poet Tony Harrison, was given the all-clear by the Independent Broadcasting Authority after it took the unusual step of showing it to the full board.

25 Originally it was to have been screened in a mid-evening slot but Channel 4 has now put it back to 11.30 p.m.
'V.', written by Harrison in
30 1985, is based on obscene grave yard graffiti and uses football hooligan slang. The title stands for 'versus' and

43

Commentary

The writers have selected emotionally loaded words to describe aspects of the poem: 'four-letter', 'filth', 'expletives', 'crudest', 'most offensive'. This generates a negative response towards the poem, though examples of the actual language used, and the context in which it is used, are not given. The reader will supply possible examples and contexts from his/her own system — for example, each reader may have his or her own candidate for 'the crudest, most offensive word', but is assumed to share the opinion of the article. The article, therefore, draws on a range of different values relating to a certain kind of language use — language that is deemed obscene — but assumes a set of shared values that the reader has no way of verifying.

This negative response to the poem is reinforced by the use of metaphor, which forces the reader to make inferences about the messages the text is carrying. The poem is described as 'a torrent of four-letter filth' and 'the cascade of expletives'. 'Torrent' and 'cascade' both give the impression of a powerful and unstoppable flow. The fact that it is a torrent of 'filth' makes the image stronger. The linking of 'filth' with fast-flowing water leads directly to images of a sewer. The article is therefore indirectly making the reader draw the inference that a TV channel is pouring sewage into people's homes, more specifically, their 'living rooms', a point that, if made directly, might be dismissed as overstatement.

The emotion required of the reader is, therefore, disgust and 'fury'.

The opposition to the broadcast apparently comes from 'the political establishment', 'outraged MPs' and 'Home Secretary Douglas Hurd'. The way in which the meaning is coded here is interesting. The use of the definite article 'the' with 'political establishment' implies a previously established group that the reader is already familiar with. This would lead the reader to assume that the Government was involved. This is reinforced by reference to 'Home Secretary Douglas Hurd'. However, the actual text makes no reference to any action or comment by the then Home Secretary, merely uses a modal verb, 'will', to imply that some related action may be requested. The phrase 'outraged MPs' apparently implies 'a lot of MPs who were outraged'. A less apparent, but probably more accurate meaning is 'those MPs who were outraged'. Later in the article, only two are mentioned.

The implication of the text is that the Government objected to the broadcast, backed by a large number of MPs, and strong action would be taken.

The subject matter of the poem is not given in the first few paragraphs of the article, but the phrase 'most explicitly sexual language' carries the implication that the subject matter of the poem will be sexually explicit. In fact (as is noted later in the article), the possibly offensive language relates to the language of graffiti and the language used by skinheads. The fact that this information is given later in the article allows the reader to generate a negative view of the broadcast before these details are given.

The readers' initial assumption may be that the subject matter of the poem is sexual.

All of these responses are generated by the use of common norms of language by which users of language negotiate meaning. In face-to-face interaction, meaning can be discussed and negotiated, the discourse can be interrupted or redirected by either or all parties involved. In the case of written text, the reader has first to identify the meanings indirectly contained within the text. Second, if the text relates to something outside the readers' immediate experience (and an as yet unbroadcast TV programme must fit this description) then the reader has no choice but to accept the information as translated through the text.

The overt role of the newspaper article is to transmit news. The analyses in the previous sections suggest that different methods of readership identification and address can be used to present information in a way that guides and directs the response of the reader by putting him/her in the role of the implied reader and creating a system of shared values that may not actually reflect the opinions of the individual members of this group. If the reader uncritically accepts the article as an item of news (and how many people read newspapers with the close critical attention that this kind of analysis requires), the implications contained within the article, and the inferences that he/she is being guided to draw from it, may be accepted at face value.

EDITORIALISING

It is easier to respond to opinion when it is open and addressed directly to the recipient as opinion rather than concealed and addressed to the recipient as fact. Editorials exist to allow the newspaper (usually in the person of its editor) to comment, give views on and draw conclusions from the day's events.

As the activity on p. 37–38 above noted, newspapers create an implied audience by overt identification in which the paper becomes an individual and the readers are a named group – *Sun* readers or *Mirror* readers. The papers mark their editorial section in a similar way. The broadsheets (who do not, as a rule, refer directly to their readers as a group) don't mark the editorial in any specific way, apart from headlining it according to topic. The tabloids identify themselves by name, and mark the editorial specifically as opinion or comment. The exception here is the *Sun* which marks its editorial as 'The Sun Says', making reference, perhaps, to the spoken voice - this paper talks to its readers.

Text: Opinions

The editorial gives a newspaper the opportunity to address its readership directly, and the editorial is the place where the reader may expect to find overt comment on the news of the day. However, the 'created' reader, the implied reader, is again in evidence as the editorial addresses a group with shared (but not always explicitly expressed) values.

Text: Liberty is from the *Daily Mail*, and refers to changes in the law relating to the rights of people who have been arrested to remain silent, and the right of asylum seekers to claim financial support while their claims are going to appeal.

Text: Liberty

What a liberty

LADIES and gentlemen of the jury, consider these two facts:

Since the Home Secretary curbed the right to silence, the number of suspects refusing to answer police questions has almost halved. Likewise, the number coming here and claiming asylum has plummeted by 50 per cent since Michael Howard insisted on preventing those of them who enter the country on false pretences from living off benefit.

Both these reforms were enacted against sustained protests from self-proclaimed libertarians. And both are now getting results which should delight law-abiding Britons who prize any enlargement of their freedom from justice-cheating crooks or foreign spongers.

The headline appeals to the reader to develop a sense of indignation or outrage – 'What a liberty' is a well-known phrase for expressing indignation against someone who has been unreasonable or disrespectful. It reflects the speaking voice, an exclamation, and the writer doesn't specify whose voice this is – maybe that of the reader as implied reader, or the newspaper as narrator, championing the cause of the reader.

The speaking voice continues, but now in the context of a law court, and the reader, who is now the member of the 'jury', is addressed by the voice of the barrister. As readers, we are given two potential roles. We can be either 'self-proclaimed libertarians' or 'law-abiding Britons'. At first glance, there seems to be some equivalence between the two groups. The structures of the phrases are identical, but the meaning is not. 'Self-proclaimed' has become a term of abuse implying doubt as to the status of the self-proclaimed individual. 'Law-abiding' has more of a factual status and clearly indicates a desirable quality. 'Libertarian', which means literally a believer in the freedom of the will, has become associated with groups that want to remove all legal restraints on personal behaviour, but there is no recognised libertarian movement. 'Britons', on the other hand, again has some factual status, and appeals to senses of patriotism. The implied reader is, therefore, a person who upholds the law and is a patriot. This person will listen with approving respect to the 'facts' that the voice of the barrister is giving. This is slightly different from the overt identification of a readership in the previous examples, but it does, in effect, push the reader into identifying with one group – the group that agrees with the editorial, and therefore shares the values of the paper.

The editorial then goes on to the facts of the argument. The 'facts' relate to the decreasing numbers of people who take their right to silence under police questioning, and the decreasing number of asylum seekers coming to Britain since changes in the law were made. These facts do have verifiable status as they contain figures that presumably can be checked, even if they are not precise – 'almost halved' and '50 per cent'. Both the reader and the implied reader can identify the factual status of these figures. However, towards the end of the report, these facts are extended without any signalling so that those arrested become 'justice-cheating crooks' and those claiming asylum in Britain (not just those appealing against refusals to grant asylum) become 'foreign spongers'.

The underlying implication here is that any person arrested and wishing to claim the right to silence is guilty, and any asylum seeker is here only to take advantage of the benefit system. The reader may, or may not share these views, but they are presented as having a factual status:

- ◎ They are presented in a factual context: 'the number . . . *has* almost halved'; 'the number . . . *has* plummeted'.
- ◎ They are presented as desirable: 'curbed the right to silence, insisted on preventing . . . false pretences'.
- ◎ The final move from the factual to the non-factual is embedded in a complex sentence that begins with a fact delivered in a statement: 'both *are* . . . getting results', moves to an opinion that appeals to the implied reader expressed through a modal verb: 'which *should* delight law-abiding Britons', and finally attaches the 'fact' to Britons' 'freedom from . . .'

THE SUN SAYS

Salute from the Poms

DOWN UNDER they are having the biggest and longest birthday party in history.

It is exactly 200 years since the first British fleet, with its mixed cargo of sheep stealers, pickpockets and naughty ladies, dropped anchor in Botany Bay.

However, there are skeletons at the feast.

"What is there to celebrate?" demand a thousand placards.

The Aussies are being asked to tear out their hearts over the plight of the poor old Abos.

They are asked to believe that, before the white man stole their land, Australia was a paradise inhabited by gentle, trusting, children of nature living on the fat of the land.

In fact, the Aboriginals were treacherous and brutal.

They had acquired none of the skills or the arts of civilisation.

They were nomads who in 40,000 years left no permenant settlements.

The history of mankind is made up of migrations. Australia no more belongs to them than England does to the Ancient Brits who painted themselves blue.

Left alone, the Abos would have wiped themselves out.

Certainly, they have suffered from the crimes (and the diseases) of the Europeans.

Tamed

That is inevitable when there is a collision between peoples at different stages of development. *The Aussies tamed a continent*.

They have built a race of tough, bloody-minded individualists.

We have had our differences — over politics and more serious things like cricket — but when the chips were down they have always proved true friends.

Not bad at all for a bunch of ex-cons!

We hope that they enjoy their long, long shindig and crack a few tubes for the Poms.

49

Activity

Read Text: Salute, which appeared in the *Sun* in January 1988, about the Australian bicentenary celebrations.

◎   What shared values is the editorial trying to promote?
◎   Who is being addressed?
◎   What 'facts' is the reader being asked to accept?
◎   How does the editorial attempt to give these factual status?

Summary

Newspapers are not simply vehicles for delivering information. They present the reader with aspects of the news, and present it often in a way that intends to guide the ideological stance of the reader. The tabloids, in particular, are very clear about their own voice (THE SUN SAYS, etc.), and a lot of the time pretend that they are addressing a coherent group of people, their own readers. The *Sun* reader, the *Mirror* reader – these groups are frequently referred to, appealed to and invoked.

The broadsheets, too, identify their own readership as some kind of homogeneous group with identical aims, beliefs and opinions. The *Guardian*, for example, is happy to satirise the popular image of its readers – a strip cartoon that appeared regularly in the *Guardian* had two young financiers discussing their future in-laws as 'Guardian readers', using this term as shorthand for 'left-wing'.

The *Independent* began its advertising with the image of its reader – the person whose views and opinions are their own – with the slogan: IT IS – ARE YOU?

The problem is that these groups don't exist in the way the papers pretend. Most people have probably read the popular tabloids, and most broadsheet readers will have read rival publications even if they have a preference for one particular one.

However, the creation of groups in this way has the effect of implying the existence of a body of opinion, and frequently opinion that is associated with qualities that the majority of people who read the articles would find desirable. There is no logical reason to assume, for example, that the 'law-abiding people' of the previous *Daily Mail* editorial form a coherent group, or even an easily identifiable group (are 'law-abiding people' those who never break the law, or does this term include people who occasionally fiddle their taxes or insurance, or who sometimes exceed the speed limit when they are driving? Different

50

people will have different views), that they all support changes to the asylum laws or to the right to silence. There is probably a very wide range of views on the subject. The editorial presented, though, equates the quality of being law-abiding with a particular attitude, and leads the reader to assume that this attitude is shared by a large number of people.

Extension

1   Collect some editorials. Can you identify a 'group' that is being addressed? What language devices are being used to create and address that group?
2   Find articles that either address the reader directly, or that identify a group such as *Sun* readers or *Mirror* readers. What values are the individual reader or these groups supposed to hold? How does the newspaper establish these values?

51

Representations of groups: words, words, words

LINGUISTIC DETERMINISM

Writers of fiction have often speculated about the role of language in the forming and maintaining of social structures and roles. George Orwell, in his book *Nineteen Eighty-Four*, postulated a society in which the ruling powers tried to maintain almost total control over the population. A weapon in this control was the language Newspeak, which contained no way of expressing concepts and ideologies that were opposed to the state. The creators of Newspeak believed that without the language to express the concepts of rebellion, rebellion would be impossible. If people didn't have the words to formulate the concept of rebellion, the theory went, then rebellion could not happen. An example that Orwell gives is the word 'good' and its opposite 'bad'. The meanings of these words can be made more exact, and less open to individual interpretation, if the opposite of 'good' becomes 'ungood'. Degrees of 'goodness' and 'ungoodness' can be expressed by the clear and strictly defined (by the state) terms 'plusungood', 'doubleplusungood', instead of the more vague 'more', 'very', 'rather', etc.

Modern research into language and mind suggests that people do not depend on language for thought. Babies can think before they have language, and adults frequently have the frustrating experience of not being able to find the words that exactly express the thought they had. Orwell's vision of a population controlled by its language is an unlikely, or even an impossible one. Language use is, anyway, so creative that a system that worked on the principle of one word = one meaning would not continue to do so for very long.

Even so, language can be a powerful tool. It is, perhaps, at its most powerful when its role in presenting the world to an audience is not explicit; in other words, it is easy to resist a particular viewpoint or ideology when you know it is being presented to you, but not so easy to resist when the viewpoint or ideology is concealed.

The unit on audience (Unit 3) looked at the way newspapers can artificially construct an audience (the implied audience), as a way of manipulating the actual audience into taking on a role or stance that they may not otherwise have taken. This section looks in more detail at the way language can be used to represent particular groups to promote particular attitudes or conform to an existing stereotype.

Certain groups tend to be disadvantaged within particular societies. People are defined by their sex, their race, their sexuality, their religion – and these groups can be disliked, feared, discriminated against or actively persecuted. Language is one of the means by which attitudes towards groups can be constructed, maintained – or challenged.

For example, some people have a physical disability. Their mobility, their sight, their hearing may be in some way impaired. These groups are often identified by their disability. They are 'the handicapped' as a general group - more specifically they are 'the blind', 'the deaf', 'the crippled'. This form of naming defines people by one aspect of themselves, and many are unhappy with this labelling, just as many people would be unhappy to be defined as 'the freckled', 'the big-nosed' or even 'the hearing' or 'the seeing'. Such labelling can create a situation in which people lose their individuality and become just their disability. Pressure to change this kind of labelling has encouraged society as a whole to reconsider their attitude to people with disabilities and has revealed a lot of unrecognised discrimination and unfairness. Many people with disabilities now reject the label 'disabled' and prefer the term 'differently abled'.

Newspapers are cultural artefacts. The print media of different countries and different cultures differ in a variety of ways. The American press, for example, has tabloid newspapers that are very different in format, and in many ways in content, from British tabloids. An American journalist, Randy Shilts, in his book chronicling the AIDS epidemic, *And The Band Played On,* made reference to 'the always hysterical British press'. This is not to say that the British press is necessarily worse or better than the press of other countries - but that whatever it is, it is a product of the culture it comes from.

This is an important point to bear in mind when dealing with the language of newspapers. Everything that is written in a newspaper has to be transmitted through the medium of language. The transmission of a message through language almost of necessity encodes values into the message. Language gathers its own emotional and cultural 'loading'. What this loading is will depend on the nature of the culture or sub-culture in which the language exists.

For example, if a particular culture has little respect for certain groups, concepts or beliefs, then the language for expressing ideas about those groups, concepts or beliefs will reflect that attitude. Therefore, when these things are written about, people reading the text will have their attitudes reinforced by the way the language presents these things to them. This is not to say that we are trapped by language. Beliefs and values change, and language changes as well. It does mean, however, that language can inhibit people from critically evaluating the opinions and views they hold – a fact much relied on by advertisers, politicians and all those whose function in life is to manipulate social attitudes.

Language operates at a series of levels. Written text has a visual or **graphological** level. Spoken text has an aural or **phonological** level, which, however, can also be exploited by written text. All texts have a word or **lexical** level, and all texts have a structural and grammatical or **syntactic** level. It is also important to remember that texts operate within a cultural context; that is, they are created within a particular culture, and operate within the value system of that culture. This unit looks at the way in which word choice can create an ideological slant towards groups.

A simple and obvious way in which language can be used to present specific ideas about a group is through the choice of words used to name and describe that group.

WHAT'S IN A NAME?

Naming is an aspect of language surrounded with social rules and pitfalls. In most cultures, it is possible to cause offence by adopting the wrong naming strategy towards people. In France, for example, the use of *tu* and *vous* operates to specific social constraints. An English speaker, using these forms as though they were equivalent to the English social rules for formal or casual address, is very likely to get them wrong, and cause offence.

55

Activity

Below is a list of possible forms of naming in English. For each one, try to identify a context in which one person might choose to address or name another in this way, and the relationship between the speakers implied by the name form chosen. You may find that each form carries more than one possible context and relationship. What attitudes can be implied by the naming strategy used?

Naming forms

First name only (e.g. Elizabeth, Robert); short form of first name only (e.g. Liz, Bob, Rob); first name + last name (e.g. Elizabeth Smart); title + last name (e.g. Ms, Mrs, Miss, Mr, Master); title only (e.g. Sir, Madam); last name only (e.g. Smart, Shaw); nickname (Di, Fergie); profession or trade (e.g. Doctor, Constable); formal title + name (Lord Archer, The Right Honourable John Major); formal title (Her Royal Highness, Madam Speaker, My Lord); anonymous address (boy, girl, you); assumed name – given by others (Maggie [Thatcher], The Comeback Kid); assumed name taken by the named individual (Sting, Snoop Doggie Dogg); other group (dearly beloved, comrades, ladies and gentlemen, girls, boys).

Context

Classroom, interview (job), interview (TV or radio), article, informal chat, ritual or ceremony, situation relating to profession or trade, other (specify).

Relationship to named individual(s)

Formal, informal, friends, relations, strangers, superior, inferior, colleagues, senior colleagues, other.

Commentary

Naming, context and relationship operate together to create a complex series of meanings. It is not possible in most cases to attach one meaning to one form of naming. For example, the terms 'Sir' and 'Madam' would tend to imply a formal relationship that may be mutual (Sir ÷ Sir). It isn't possible to say whether the participants know each other as this form can be used whether they do or not. These forms can also imply an imbalance (Sir or Madam ÷ first name). It can also be used in situations where the power balance is not in favour of the person addressed as 'Sir'. The police may address a member of the public as 'Sir', even though they may be planning to arrest or question that person. The use of 'boy' or 'girl' implies an adult to child relationship and, when used by one adult to another, can be deeply offensive.

The use of nicknames can indicate friendship and affection, though imposed nicknames can indicate that the namer feels that he/she has the right to impose a label on the named.

Looked at fairly simply, it is possible to generalise to a certain extent. From the point of view of the addressee, being addressed by first name only suggests either equal status or inferior status, title and last name suggests a formal situation or superior status, short form of first name suggests friendship, nicknames suggest close friendship, formal title suggests superior status, a ritual form suggests participation in a particular ritual (a court hearing, a parliamentary debate), as does specific group naming.

However, the system of naming can be manipulated to create very specific effects.

Activity

Look again at the article 'Four-Letter TV Poem Fury', discussed on pp. 44–45. This time the full article is reproduced.

◎   How are those opposed to the broadcast named?
◎   How are those in support of or associated with the broadcast named?
◎   Does the naming influence the attitude the reader might take to the production?

Commentary

A clear pattern emerges when the naming strategies used in this article are looked at. Those who oppose the broadcast are given their full names: 'Gerald Howarth', 'Teddy Taylor', 'Mary Whitehouse'. They are also given their titles where appropriate: 'Tory MP Gerald Howarth . . . Teddy Taylor'. They are, therefore, accorded respect in the context of the article.

Those supporting the broadcast are named differently. The poet Tony Harrison is given his full name once, and a form of title 'Newcastle

57

Text: Poem fury

FOUR-LETTER TV POEM FURY

By JOHN DEANS and GARRY JENKINS

BROADCASTERS are lining up for a head-on clash with the political establishment over a planned Channel 4 programme featuring a
5 **torrent of fourletter filth.**

Outraged MPs last night demanded an immediate ban on the screening, which will unleash the most explicitly sexual language yet beamed into the nation's living rooms.

10 And the pressure will be on Home Secretary Douglas Hurd, who is proposing to set up a new watchdog Broadcasting Standards Council, to crack down on the media bosses now.

The cascade of expletives will pour out to viewers at the rate of
15 two a minute during the 45-minute show on November 4. The crudest, most offensive word is used 17 times.

The programme, a filmed recital of a poem called 'V,' written and read by Newcastle
20 poet Tony Harrison, was given the all-clear by the Independent Broadcasting Authority after it took the unusual step of showing it to the full board.

25 Originally it was to have been screened in a mid-evening slot but Channel 4 has now put it back to 11.30 p.m.
'V.', written by Harrison in
30 1985, is based on obscene grave yard graffiti and uses football hooligan slang. The title stands for 'versus' and

58

35 when published in an antho-
logy of the poet's work it was
dedicated to miners' leader
Arthur Scargill.

Last night Tory MP Gerald
Howarth called for the pro-
40 gramme to be withdrawn.

'This is another clear case of
the broadcasters trying to
assault the public by pushing
against the barriers of what is
45 acceptable, on the basis that
the more effing and blinding
they can get into everyday
programmes, the better.'

Mr Howarth, who last year
50 won a major legal battle with
the BBC over claims that
Fascists had infiltrated the
Tory Party, described 50-year-
old Harrison as 'another pro-
55 bable Bolshie poet seeking to
impose his frustrations on the
rest of us.'

Another Tory MP, Teddy
Taylor, also appealed to
60 Channel 4 chiefs to see sense.

'Obviously Channel 4 is the
place for experiment, and for a
bit of variety, but a poem
stuffed full of obscenities is
65 clearly so objectionable that it
will lead to the Government
being forced to take action it
would prefer not to have to
take,' he added.
70 And clean-up campaigner

Mary Whitehouse said: 'The
sooner the Government brings
broadcasting under the
obscenity laws, the better for
75 everyone and particularly the
public.

But 'V.' was defended by
the poet, the IBA and
Channel 4.
80 Harrison said: 'The language is an integral part of the
poem. It is the language of the
football hooligan and is seen
and heard every day.'
85 'I don't see that it should
merit any fuss whatsoever.'

The IBA said the film had
been viewed by the board at
the request of Director-
90 General John Whitney.

A spokesman said: 'It was
considered very carefully,
especially given our statutory
duty as far as matters of taste
95 and decency are concerned.
But we came to the view that
it was acceptable.'

A Channel 4 spokesman
said: 'We stand by our de-
100 cision, which was taken after
careful consideration and full
discussion with the IBA.'

But he accepted that the
film 'may be disturbing to
105 some', and a warning will be
given to viewers before it is
shown.

poet Tony Harrison', though this title does not recognise the fact that Tony Harrison is an internationally respected poet. Later in the article he is named as 'Harrison', an address that, in the context of full titles, suggests inferior status, or at least less respect. When Gerald Howarth is mentioned a second time, he is named as 'Mr Howarth', not 'Howarth'.

Others supporting the broadcast are anonymous: 'a spokesman', 'a Channel 4 spokesman'. The overall effect is to reduce the status of the supporters of the broadcast, by using naming strategies that imply that they are either inferior or anonymous.

Naming is, therefore, a very useful device in promoting a particular response from an audience. In the case of the article looked at in the last activity, naming is one device used to 'slant' a text in a particular direction in relation to an issue – the broadcast of a programme – and more widely, to promote the view that certain television channels need controlling to stop them broadcasting 'obscene' or 'corrupting' material.

Another way in which naming can be used to create a particular ideology is in promoting attitudes towards particular social groups.

NAMING OF GROUPS

Within a particular culture, the rules for naming can be complex, and the selection that a particular text makes from the possible names it can give to a group can, as the analysis above suggests, be very important in transmitting ideological values to the reader of the text.

Activity

Look again at Text: Salute (p. 49). Do the names used for the three groups mentioned carry the same connotations? Do these terms give a favourable or unfavourable picture of each group?

Group	Name
Australians	Aussies, Europeans
British	Brits, Europeans
Pre-colonials	Abos, Aboriginals

Commentary

At first glance, the terms seem equivalent. The short forms ('Aussies', 'Brits', 'Abos') are nicknames that suggest an affectionate irreverence. However, in the cultural context – that of white supremacy and colonialism – the terms do not have, and cannot be used with, equivalent values.

'Aussie' and 'Brit' both name groups that have a nationality – Australian and British. 'Abo' implies statelessness. The term 'Aussie' seems to be being used within an historical context that suggests that only the descendants of the first European settlers are included within the term. Are the descendants of the people who were already there when the settlers arrived not also nationals?

'Aboriginal' is originally an adjective meaning 'first or earliest known'; or 'earlier than European colonists'. The noun 'Aborigines' came into the language as travel and colonial expansion began, used to refer both to pre-colonial groups and to animals and plants. It therefore carries strong connotations of 'primitive', 'underdeveloped' and possibly 'sub-human'. The word 'Aboriginal' gradually developed a specialised meaning that referred directly to the pre-colonial inhabitants of Australia, but by its very nature it implies that this group belongs more to other, non-specified, pre-colonial inhabitants of various countries than it does to the country its members inhabit. In other words, it is a term loaded with value judgements.

All three short forms can be used as terms of abuse. However, it is a feature within groups that terms of abuse relating to the group can be exchanged within the group (for example, it is sometimes acceptable for the term 'nigger' to be used within the Afro-Caribbean community, whereas it is completely unacceptable outside that group). In the context of the editorial, the British and the Australians belong to the same group – Europeans. In this context, the term 'Abo' then becomes a term of abuse.

The importance and significance of naming in social groups

The importance of naming can be seen in the way that oppressed or disadvantaged groups within a society try to take control of the naming strategies that that society takes towards them. This can be seen in the black community, particularly in America, where the term 'Negro', largely adopted by white Americans as the acceptable naming form, was firmly rejected by the community and terms such as 'person of colour', 'black', 'Afro-Caribbean', and 'African-American' were used in a community forced to name itself, and perhaps to avoid the unacceptable grouping of all non-whites into an apparently homogeneous group called 'coloured' or 'black'.

As the activity above suggests, naming probably becomes less important once a group achieves equal status not just in the law, but in actuality. In Australia, the pre-colonial peoples are still seriously disadvantaged. Naming matters.

Attributes, roles and qualities

The naming strategies adopted by a text can, therefore, have a direct effect on the ideological slant of the text. A further aspect of word choice is the way in which groups are described. Description can appear as part of the naming strategy – to call someone a 'man' or a 'boy' or a 'Brit' is descriptive. Description can also be added by modification in the noun phrase (p. 20) and by the use of adjectives. In the article 'Four-Letter TV Poem Fury', Tony Harrison is described as 'another *probable Bolshie* poet', the use of the modifying phrase 'probable Bolshie' adding descriptive detail that adds to the image of the poet that the writer of the article is trying to create.

Activity

Look again at Text: Salute. What descriptive detail is given about the participants? What attributes and qualities do they have?

Commentary

The Aboriginals are described as being 'treacherous and brutal'. The qualities 'gentle' and 'trusting' are mentioned as being falsely attributed to them by others. The descriptions contained in the naming compare the Aboriginals to 'children', and 'Ancient Brits who painted themselves blue'. These descriptions portray either the concept of the savage – a sub-human species; or the noble savage – a sub-human species with a child-like innocence. Both of these representations are caricatures that are rooted in early colonialism.

The white Australians, on the other hand, are 'tough' and 'bloody-minded'. They are named as 'individualists', a description that contrasts strongly with the portrayal of the Aboriginals.

Therefore, closely linked to naming are the attributes and qualities that groups or individual members of groups are credited (or discredited) with when they are discussed in newspaper texts. Newspapers are artefacts of the dominant cultural norm, as discussed in Unit 1 (Introduction). The attitudes of the dominant culture tend to be reflected in the language of news stories, particularly those about minority power groups.

REPRESENTATIONS OF WOMEN

The following articles appeared in the press in the summer of 1996. They all have women as their central figure, but the only other criterion in the selection process was that they should not be 'glamour' items: beauty, fashion or page three texts. What words are used to refer to women in these stories? What impression does the text give in relation to the roles these women play and the qualities they have?

You might find it useful to look at:

◎ Direct naming
◎ Use of modifiers in noun phrases
◎ Adjectival description
◎ Choice of verbs to describe actions and processes attributed to these women

Women are named in these texts in an informal or casual way – 'Camilla', 'Diana', 'Glenda', 'Lisa', 'June'. In two cases, a familiar term of address, a nickname or short form, is used – 'Angie', 'Fergie'. Two women are also referred to by names of the parts they play rather than initially by their real names: 'Cindy', 'street Maxine'.

This use of familiar forms of naming, extending to naming actors by the parts they play, is not confined to women. *EastEnders* actor Brian Croucher, who plays Ted Hills in the series once said, 'Nobody calls me Brian any more. It's EastEnders or Ted.' Tabloid newspapers tend to adopt a familiar, informal approach to the majority of people who appear in their stories. However, male politicians are less likely to be referred to by their first names ('Major' and 'Blair' rather than 'John' and 'Tony').

The naming strategies adopted sometimes serve to make the woman anonymous other than in her role in relation to her situation, her family or her husband – 'Victim', 'a stalker's victim', 'Spencer's sad wife', 'the wife of Earl Spencer', 'Express chief's wife', 'the wife of a senior executive at Express Newspapers', 'the proud mum', 'a mum'. In the article about women taking up work in the construction industry, women are twice referred to as 'girls'.

Information given by modification in noun phrases, and by adjectival description, tends again to cast women in a limited series of

63

Text: Women (1)

LONG MAY SHE REIN!

Charles buys his Camilla an £8,000 grey mare

EXCLUSIVE

By WAYNE FRANCIS
Royal Reporter

PRINCE Charles has spent more than £8,000 on a horse for mistress Camilla Parker Bowles.

Charles, 47, bought grey mare Gipsy Girl as a surprise — after he had to miss Camilla's 49th birthday two weeks ago.

The Prince — on official visits in Brunei and America — was bitterly disappointed and vowed to make it up to her.

He sent an aide to Ireland to view the 17-hand high mare being sold by a breeder in Co Kilkenny.

He beat the price down from £11,000, paying £7,800 cash plus about £1,200 for transport.

The five-year-old mare was shipped to England last week and hidden in stables in the West Country until Charles could surprise his lover.

He had the horse thoroughly checked over. A Royal pal said: "Camilla is not a great rider and the Prince wanted to be sure

Camilla

Continued from Page One
it was suitable. Let's just say her enthusiasm exceeds her skill."

Camilla, who rides with the smart country set at the Beaufort Hunt, told pals she was thrilled with the present.

It is one of a string of gifts exchanged during the pair's long romance.

Charles recently gave Camilla a big spending status symbol when he ordered her a platinum American Express card.

And Camilla gave him her terrier pup Freddy after his much-loved pet Pooh vanished while hunting rabbits.

It was their gift-swapping which first sparked trouble with Princess Di.

She was furious when Camilla gave Charles a pair of cuff-links bearing intertwined 'C's as a wedding gift.

CINDY'S NAPPY ENDING

PICTURE EXCLUSIVE

STUNNING *EastEnders* star Michelle Collins showed off her beautiful baby girl for the first time yesterday – and I was the only one there to see it.

The proud mum took out baby Loulou in a trendy sling to get a breath of fresh air.

And it was great to see the star – who plays evil Cindy Beale in the BBC1 soap – and her tot looking so well.

Michelle, 32, has stayed inside her north London home since the birth after striking a deal with *OK! Weekly* magazine.

First

I'm told she is expected to earn £60,000 for the first pictures of her baby – but *Daily Mirror* readers got there first.

Michelle and Loulou were joined by a mystery male pal. There was no sign of the star's Italian lover Fabrizio Tassallini who flew to London last month for the birth.

"Michelle is feeling great and is really enjoying being a mum," said her pal.

"She's really proud of Loulou and can't stop grinning at her."

Last week millions of viewers saw Michelle's screen husband Ian, actor Adam Woodyatt, gunned down by a hitman she hired.

STREET MAXINE'S DRIVE BAN CUT SO SHE CAN FIGHT ANOREXIA

Star saved from 'hardship'

By JAN DISLEY

CORONATION Street star Tracy Shaw was yesterday saved from a six month driving ban . . . by the slimmers' disease anorexia.

Tracy, the soap's sexy Maxine Heavey, begged to be allowed to keep her licence so she could drive to counselling sessions that help her fight the illness.

And magistrates decided she would suffer "exceptional hardship" if they ordered the full six-month disqualification she was set to get.

Instead they banned her for two months and fined her £40.

The 23-year-old actress, slender in a navy suit and green silk blouse, admitted speeding at 52mph in her white VW Polo through a 40mph zone in Buxton, Derbyshire, last August.

She faced a ban after three earlier motoring offences left her with nine points on her licence.

Tracy's lawyer John Sutcliffe said: "Anorexia is a problem that's been with her for some time.

"Happily she is coming to terms with it. There is good reason to believe that with counselling and other support she is going to be able to conquer it in the very near future."

Topless

But counselling took place in Derby and she needed to live at home with her parents in Belper because their presence was central to her fight against the "tragic and debilitating" illness, he said.

If she was banned her only option would be to look for accommodation near the ITV show's Manchester studios, Mr Sutcliffe added.

"That would be a disaster as far as as her attempts to get over the illness are concerned," he said.

Rear Of The Year Tracy, who will appear topless in a magazine next month, told Buxton court she is recovering from anorexia.

"I've suffered from this condition for a couple of years now," she said.

"I've been to see a number of counsellors. This one is really helping me. I'll continue to go there until I feel strong enough to manage on my own."

Tracy, paid £50,000 a year, admitted having anorexia several months ago after she was stopped for shoplifting.

"It's very much an image thing," she said at the time. "You have to be thin.

"It's like another voice in your head telling you not to eat."

'Killer' nurses must die, say angry family

THE entire family of tragic nurse Yvonne Gilford are demanding the death penalty for two British women accused of her murder.

Yvonne's relatives voted unanimously to condemn Deborah Parry, 41, and Lucille McLauchlan, 31.

Even neighbours in Jamestown, Australia, want the pair beheaded by the Saudis if guilty. A plea for mercy could see them jailed instead.

Yvonne's brother Frank said: "The law should fit the crime." Parry, from Alton, Hants, and McLauchlan, from Dundee, earlier withdrew their confessions.

Express chief's wife arrested on suspicion of stealing Fergie book

Nick Varley

THE fierce battle for circulation between mid-market tabloid newspapers took a fresh twist yesterday when police confirmed they had arrested the wife of a senior executive at Express Newspapers on suspicion of theft.

Anita Monk, married to the Express's deputy editor Ian Monk, was detained at an hotel at Heathrow airport in possession of a pre-publication copy of a damning biography of the Duchess of York.

A second copy of the book, Fergie: Her Secret Life, which the rival Daily Mail was serialising after paying a reported £170,000 to the publisher, was later found at her home.

The duchess tried to have the book banned but had to give up after she was ordered to lodge £500,000 before her legal action could go ahead. When she failed, a fierce battle broke out over it between the Express and the Daily Mail. The Mail ran extracts of book, which included claims that the duchess would have killed herself but for her daughters, as "the book she tried to ban".

But on the first day of the Mail's serialisation, November 2, the Express also ran a story with many of the same revelations, which, the Express told its readers, had been published by a US magazine.

The previous day Mrs Monk had been arrested at Heathrow.

A police spokesman said: "A woman aged 52 was arrested on suspicion of theft and handling stolen goods.

"Officers seized from the woman a copy of a book yet to be published and another copy was seized at her home. It was Fergie: Her Secret Story. The woman was taken to Uxbridge police station and bailed to return on 18 November pending further inquiries."

A spokeswoman for Express Newspapers said: "Ian said he was not available to comment on this."

GLENDA TO FIGHT ON THE BEACHES

LABOUR will be fighting for votes on the beaches of Spain tomorrow.

Shadow Transport Minister Glenda Jackson will hand out sticks of rock to holidaymakers in Benidorm and Alicante.

I lay wide awake as docs cut me open

Mum June's op hell

By SYDNEY YOUNG

A MUM who had a heart attack during major surgery claimed yesterday that she was WIDE AWAKE when doctors operated.

June Blacker said she suffered agonising pain from the scalpel because the anaesthetic hadn't worked.

Now June, whose heart stopped for **THREE MINUTES**, is suing health chiefs over her horror ordeal. "It was every patient's worst nightmare," she said.

The 43-year-old catering worker, who was in hospital to be sterilised, couldn't raise the alarm because she had been given muscle-relaxing drugs.

ORDEAL: Mum June

A STUNNING pal of comedy star John Cleese miraculously escaped death yesterday when her plane careered through an airfield fence at 100mph and was rammed by a van.

The £1million Lear jet carrying 27-year-old Lisa Hogan broke in two as it shot across a packed main road.

Terrified drivers braked and swerved, fearing a fireball.

But as a waterfall of fuel poured from the plane's shattered wing tanks, 6ft 2in Lisa coolly climbed from a smashed window.

A stunned witness to the crash on the A40 at Northolt, West London, said: "We found her sitting on a wall. All she wanted was a cigarette."

The Irish-born beauty, who stars with Cleese in his new film Fierce Creatures, was treated in hospital for a cut leg.

Women wanted for building site work

by **JOHN INGHAM**
Environment Correspondent

And it's not just so we can whistle at 'em, say bosses

BRITAIN'S most sexist industry has been told to recruit women — or risk a manpower crisis.

Construction chiefs are being urged to shed their macho image to make room for female brickies.

And wolf-whistling at pretty girls could be a thing of the past among tomorrow's female scaffolders.

Many firms already report a shortage of skilled electricians and joiners. Now there are fears that a drop in the birth rate 20 years ago means that there will not be enough young men to fill the jobs.

Industry bosses will be told to make construction more attractive to women by providing all-girl training courses, flexi-time and proper childcare facilities.

The move could lead to creches on building sites once dominated by hairy, beer-swilling men with tattoos.

Sexy pin-ups would almost certainly be banned to make women feel more "comfortable" in the workplace.

And women's support groups to rival the old boy's network could be introduced.

The shake-up will be formally recommended by the Government-sponsored Construction Industry Board next month.

A CIB survey has found that schoolchildren think the industry is "dirty, dangerous and demoralised".

A CIB source warned: "If the industry fails to respond to the report's recommendations to recruit more women it will face increasing skill shortages and problems with recruitment.

"Demographic changes and the increasing success of women in both education and employment will mean that employers will face a shrinking number of applications from young men.

"We are not calling for women to be hired to be politically correct.

"It is a question of productivity and necessity in an industry increasingly hit by skill shortages.

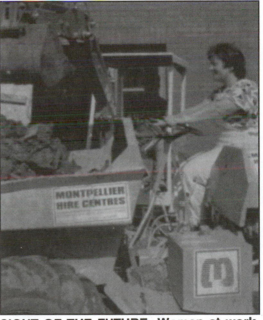

SIGHT OF THE FUTURE: Women at work

"The industry should realise it is ignoring half the country's workforce by not recruiting women. But why shouldn't women work as bricklayers or electricians?"

The construction industry has an unenviable reputation for sexism. CIB figures show it has the lowest proportion of women employees of any mainline British industry.

Women make up 46 per cent of Britain's working population but only 10 per cent of the construction industry — and most of them are secretaries or clerks.

Not only are fewer women recruited but their drop-out rate is higher than the men's — possibly because of the macho lifestyle.

The battered huts of building sites are notorious for their explicit pin-ups and the crude jokes of their occupants.

The CIB wants "mentoring and support" schemes for women to stop them feeling isolated.

Diana breaks taboo to upstage the Queen

by ROBERT JOBSON Royal Correspondent

IT is the unwritten royal rule — one never upstages a tour by the Queen.

But yesterday Princess Diana did just that in what some will see as an act of pique over being stripped of her HRH title.

She announced a trip to Australia which clashes with the Queen's major tour of the year to Thailand.

The Queen's state visit is at the invitation of King Bhumibol to celebrate his 50th year on the throne. She will be accompanied by the Duke of Edinburgh.

The centrepiece comes on October 31 when Her Majesty lays a wreath at the memorial to Second World War veterans.

On the same day Diana will step out at a fund-raising dinner in aid of cancer research in Sydney and is bound to steal the headlines.

Last night Diana's officials insisted the Princess had the Queen's blessing for her trip. One source said: "In accordance to the divorce agreement she sought Her Majesty's permission for this trip to Australia. The Queen gave permission." However, sources inside the Palace said there is some "disquiet" over the Princess's plans.

"It has always been the custom that nobody makes alternative foreign tours when the Queen is on an official State visit abroad," one said. "The Princess has clearly chosen to ignore that unwritten rule.

"Obviously, the Queen would not want to make things difficult for the Princess when she is carrying out charitable work abroad.

"The Palace has known about the Princess's plans for the last two months. She has changed the dates once already."

Fears for Spencer's sad wife

From NICK PARKER in Cape Town, South Africa

THE wife of Earl Spencer has been "badly hurt" by his friendship with a pal's missus, friends said last night.

The romance between the 31-year-old Earl — Princess Di's brother — and married beauty Chantal Collopy, 37, was a "shattering blow" they said.

And they spoke of their fears for waif-like ex-model Victoria, 29, who has battled eating disorders and depression. One said: "Victoria has tried hard to put a brave face on things but she has been badly hurt.

"She only leaves the house to shop and is detached and isolated."

Sad Victoria — mum of Earl Spencer's four children — spent yesterday shut inside her Cape Town mansion.

Friends say she looks healthy but remains painfully thin. The Earl moved her and the kids to South Africa for a "fresh start" in January.

Chantal's spurned husband Don, 41, is suing Spencer for £22,000 for stealing his wife.

Victim weeps as stalking ex-love freed

By STEPHEN WHITE

A STALKER'S victim wept yesterday as the man who has tormented her for 18 months walked free.

Waitress Gabrielle Hart's life turned into a nightmare after she ended a year-long romance with jobless trucker Barry Wright.

He plagued her with phone calls, tried to run her down with his motorbike and even attempted suicide in her driveway. Once 30-year-old Wright told her: "If I can't have you, I'll kill you."

But when he appeared in court in Wigan, Lancs., yesterday, Wright was let off with 18 months probation.

After the case Gabrielle, 22, said: "I can't believe he has been allowed to go free. I cannot see an end to this nightmare. The law needs to be changed."

Her father John said: "This man is a menace. He shouldn't be out on the streets."

Menace

He admitted assault, dangerous driving, making malicious phone calls and criminal damage.

roles: mothers – '*mum* June'; in relation to men – '*his* Camilla', '*mistress* Camilla Parker Bowles'; in relation to physical appearance – '*stunning* Michelle Collins', '*sexy* Maxine', '*pretty* girls', 'married *beauty*'; and as victims: 'Spencer's *sad* wife', '*waif-like* Victoria'. Women are sometimes described in relation to their careers 'Overseas Development Minister Clare Short', but this is infrequent.

In the examples looked at, many women perform no actions at all, but are on the receiving end of the actions of others: 'they had arrested the wife of . . .'; 'Prince Charles has spent more than £8,000 on a horse for mistress Camilla Parker Bowles'; 'Britain's most sexist industry has been told to recruit women'; 'Construction chiefs are being urged . . . to make room for female brickies'. Some of the actions attributed to women in the articles have connotations of child-like behaviour: 'showed off', 'upstage'. The use of 'upstage' in the article relating to the Princess of Wales plays on the image of women as rivals, and the Princess's act is explicitly described as 'an act of pique' (definition: ill-feeling, resentment, hurt pride). Where women are seen to act more positively, it is often against their own bodies and emotions. Tracy Shaw 'fights' anorexia, Victoria Spencer 'battles' eating disorders and depression. Lisa Hogan, exceptionally, 'escapes' and 'coolly climbs out'.

A random selection of stories suggests that certain stereotypes are operating in the press in relation to women. There is a tendency to depict them as existing primarily in relation to their families – their children, their husbands or partners rather than as individuals in their own right. Younger women are frequently described in relation to their physical appearance. Women are often depicted as weaker – they are victims, they are on the receiving end of action rather than the performers of it. If this selection is representative, then the newspaper-reading public receives a series of images depicting women according to a very limiting stereotype that values them in only a narrow set of roles.

SEXUALITY

Within our society, there is often seen to be one acceptable norm for behaviour. Groups that do not conform to this norm are often stigmatised, a clear example being the gay community. This group has been fighting for equality of legislation which once saw all male homosexual acts as illegal, then saw such acts as legal between consenting males over the age of 21 in private and, very recently, as legal between consenting males over 18 in private. Despite modification of the legislation, there is still a lot of hostility towards homosexuality in our

69

culture, boosted by the AIDS epidemic that has been seen as an affliction of the gay community in Britain and the USA. Is this hostility evident in newspaper articles involving the gay community?

Activity

The following articles appeared on the front and inside pages of the *Sun* on 6 January 1997. They concern a story that broke in the *News of the World* the previous day, claiming that a Tory MP had had a homosexual relationship with a young man who was below the age of legal consent at the time the relationship was said to have taken place (the age of legal consent for homosexual relationships is now 18, as opposed to 16 for heterosexual relationships, but at the time the relationship was said to have taken place, it was 21). The first article was a front page story, and the second occupied a two-page spread on the inside pages. Only the first few paragraphs of each article are reproduced.

How are gays depicted in these articles? Does the word choice promote a particular ideological stance towards the gay community? You may find it helpful to look at:

◎   Naming
◎   Modification and adjectival description
◎   Use of metaphor
◎   Use of word play (e.g. puns)
◎   Choice of verbs to describe actions and processes attributed to the two men in the centre of this story, and the response of others involved

Commentary

The articles show different attitudes towards the gay community – or possibly just to this story. The first focuses on the political repercussions. Mr Hayes is linked to the gay community by the use of noun phrase modification in the headline: 'gay fling MP Jerry'. In the article itself, Mr Hayes is named largely by his role as an MP – 'Tory MP Jerry Hayes', 'the 43-year-old MP', with modification giving information about his age and his status.

The young man who alleges Mr Hayes had an affair with him, Paul Stone, is named three times, once anonymously as 'an under-age boy' and twice by given name with very little modification or adjectival

Text: Fling

Gay fling MP Jerry in fight to keep job

By TREVOR KAVANAGH
Political Editor

TORY MP Jerry Hayes was fighting for his political life last night after bosses ordered a showdown over his gay affair with an under-age boy.

Angry voters in the married barrister's Essex constituency urged him to quit at the next election.

And ministers were counting on the local party to order him out.

But senior Tory members were battling to save the 43-year-old MP — and friends inside the party privately backed him.

Letters

The storm broke after ex-student Paul Stone claimed he had a 16-month affair with the member for Harlow.

Stone — who produced graphic love letters — was then 18. The legal age of consent was 21.

description – 'ex-student Paul Stone', 'Stone'. The description only gives his age at the time the affair was said to have happened. Others involved are named in political terms – 'voters', 'ministers', 'senior Tory members'.

The article uses words from the **semantic field** (area of meaning) of battle to place this story in its political context – 'MP in fight', 'Jerry Hayes was fighting for his ... life', 'showdown', 'senior Tory members were battling'; and one phrase from the field of weather, that is often used in the context of war – 'the storm broke'. As well as producing powerful description, this creates metaphor that emphasises the potential damage this story could do. The political scene becomes a battleground, an appropriate image in an election year.

The second article from the *Sun* goes on to demonstrate exactly

71

Text: Love poem

PERVY JERRY'S POEM OF LOVE TO GAY BOY

'I'll give you my best'

TORY MP Jerry Hayes sent his gay toyboy a Valentine's card containing a slushy poem which pledged: "I promise to love you in good times and in bad."

Hayes, 43, signed the card he gave to teenager Paul Stone with a single kiss.

By AIDAN McGURRAN

The poem, by Dorothy R Colgan, is called My Promise Of Love To You and contains the line: "I promise to give you the best of myself."

It adds: "I fell in love with you for the qualities, abilities and outlook on life that you have."

Hayes sent the card to Stone in 1992. It was in an envelope franked in the House of Commons. The lad was then 18 — at a time when the legal age of consent for homosexuals was still 21.

Their 16-month affair took place when the MP, who is married with two children, was on an IRA hit list.

Security chiefs found the list during a raid in Ulster.

Threat

Hayes' name appeared together with other prominent Tories and senior members of the Armed Forces.

The fling with former Young Conservative Paul could have left Hayes vulnerable to blackmail attempts by the Provos.

The MP was targeted by the IRA after he became a Parliamentary aide to Northern Ireland minister Robert Atkins.

Eight police marksmen guarded his family home in Wenden's Ambo, Essex, round the clock for three months.

His garage doors were bomb-proofed. And behind them armed cops secretly set up a control room watching all approaches to the property.

An ex-cop who was responsible for the MP's security said yesterday: "We took the threat very seriously indeed."

Paul told The Sun's sister paper the News of the World how Hayes got him a House of Commons security pass by claiming he was his unpaid researcher.

He said the MP often chatted to him about Ulster. Paul added: "When I joked to him that I could blow up the House of Commons he just ignored me."

Paul, now 24, said he first met Hayes at a gay rights group meeting.

Hours later they committed a lewd sex act in a park, it was claimed.

Paul, who was studying for his A-levels at the time, said Hayes also wined and dined him at expensive restaurants.

Magic

Hayes, vice chairman of the Commons AIDS committee, also sent Paul intimate letters on Commons notepaper.

One read: "I love you. I miss the magic of your hugs and watching you when you are asleep."

Another declared: "Just remember, 1 We love each other **VERY** much. 2 We miss each other **VERY** much. 3 We have fun together and can help each other."

Paul had access to virtually every area of Westminster.

He said: "Jerry liked having me around for when the mood took him, which was quite a lot. I was being introduced to people like Michael Portillo and Virginia Bottomley."

He said Hayes always professed to be devoted to his wife Alison, 40, and their children aged seven and nine.

Hayes' political career has been coloured by a string of game-for-a-laugh stunts on TV.

He has dressed up as a bumble bee, sky-dived in a chicken costume — and was even whipped in kinky bondage gear on a late-night show.

what kind of political damage such a story can do. This article focuses much more on the gay aspects of the story. Mr Hayes is named in the headline as 'Pervy Jerry', and Mr Stone is 'gay boy', 'his gay toyboy'. The use of 'boy' both emphasises the point that Mr Stone was legally under age at the time but also reduces and demeans him. The implications of 'boy' as a naming term are discussed in the section on naming above (pp. 55–57). 'Pervy' is a word that is new in the English language, appearing in the most recent edition of the *Oxford Dictionary*. It came into the language via a well-established route, that of shortening existing words. It carries the meaning of 'sexually perverted', and in this context carries two implications: firstly that Mr Hayes is a sexual pervert, and secondly that homosexual behaviour is abnormal.

This concept of homosexual behaviour as abnormal is carried through the story via the word choice. A love poem is 'slushy'. They are said to have 'committed', a verb normally associated with criminal activity, 'a lewd sex act' together. This word choice carries strong connotations of illegal and abnormal behaviour. There is also an element of belittlement in the use of idioms such as 'caught with their trousers down', 'caught with his pants down', that have connotations of a stage farce. These, combined with words such as 'slushy' and 'toyboy', refuse to recognise the possibility of serious emotional involvement in such a relationship.

Activity

The article in the *Express* relates to the same story about Jerry Hayes. How does this paper represent the gay community?

Summary

Word choice is a powerful tool for establishing an ideological stance. The examples discussed in this unit show the way in which the beliefs and prejudices of a society can be reinforced by language use that supports an existing belief system. The use of belittling, demeaning or derogatory terms towards a disadvantaged group can help to promote the belief that the group itself is to blame for its disadvantage – the Aboriginals deserved to lose their land, women are weak and can have only a limited number of roles; and gays are foolish or cunning perverts. Very few people would agree with these statements, but many would read these views expressed in newspaper articles without challenging

BOY WHO DRAGGED DOWN A TORY MP

BY LEWIS SMITH AND PAUL CROSBIE

THESE are the eyes that captured the heart of Tory MP Jerry Hayes.

As our exclusive picture shows, theatrical Paul Stone loves to dress up as a woman, at least on stage.

Last night pressure was growing on father-of-two Mr Hayes to resign following claims that the pair had a 16-month relationship.

The MP is alleged to have written: "I know by looking into your eyes that you really loved me too."

In his garish, multi-coloured wig, Tory activist and gay rights supporter Mr Stone looks just the part as Widow Scratchitt in Sinbad the Sailor. He is seen here in rehearsal for a church hall production in Peterborough last year.

But the stage was not the only place he enjoyed appearing with face paint. On a number of occasions he shocked Tory workers by turning up at political meetings wearing make-up.

Details of his colourful life emerged as the Prime Minister attempted to play down the latest embarrassment to the Conservatives, who are launching a new family values campaign.

Mr Stone is believed to have pocketed £100,000 for his "kiss and tell" story in a downmarket newspaper.

Westminster insiders are convinced it is no coincidence that details of the relationship have emerged in the run-up to the election.

Mr Stone was chairman of Peterborough Young Conservatives and met Mr Hayes, MP for Harlow, at the 1991 Conservative Party Conference in Blackpool.

"He's not the angel he makes out to be," said a friend. "He probably sees telling about his

PAGE 3 COLUMN 1

Text: Revenge

Revenge of the little mummy's boy

them, because the views are not expressed overtly, but concealed in the word choice.

Extension

1   Look at the way members of minority power groups are named in newspapers of other cultures and countries – America or Australia, for example.
2   Identify a story that focuses on a woman. Compare the naming strategies used for this woman, and the qualities and attributes she

is described as having. Is there any difference between the tabloid and the broadsheet newspapers here? How do the mid-range tabloids employ naming strategies?

3   Analyse news stories in the *Sun* from the 1992 and 1997 general elections. Compare the representation of Neil Kinnock and Margaret Thatcher with that of Tony Blair and John Major.

Representations of groups: syntax

This section will look at some of the ways in which larger units of language can be used to represent social groups and to promote a dominant cultural norm. The aspects that will be discussed in some detail are **syntax**, which deals with word order and the relationships that exist between elements in a clause.

Syntax is an important factor in the way a text creates meaning. The way in which elements within a clause are ordered can give weighting to one or more aspects, and reduce, or remove, others. The relationship between elements has a fundamental role here. This unit will look at the way these relationships work.

In traditional grammars, verbs are often defined as 'doing words', that is, as actions. Anyone who has tried to label word classes using this definition will have found that it is not really very helpful, as the following sentences demonstrate. The verbs are highlighted.

1   Cindy **was** stunning.
2   Pamela **reported** her son to the authorities.
3   Police **arrested** Paula Yates yesterday.
4   Paula Yates **went** voluntarily yesterday to Chelsea police station.
5   The ex-supermodel **weighs** ten stone.
6   Madonna **is** a mum!

Some of these verbs could be described as actions – 'arrested', 'went', 'reported' – but the others don't really fit that definition. 'Is', 'was', 'weighs' refer more to states and processes.

Some of the verbs establish a relationship between two people or groups of people: Pamela and her son; the police and Paula Yates. Both parties are involved in the process: Pamela performed the action of reporting, the object or target of her action is her son. The police have caused an action to occur – they have performed an action. The person affected by that action is Paula Yates.

In the other cases, only one person is involved in the process: Cindy, Paula Yates, the ex-supermodel, Madonna. One of these verbs refers to an action – 'went' – but this action does not involve anyone else. The other verbs refer to states, and create a relationship between a person and a condition: 'Cindy' and 'stunning'; 'the ex-supermodel' and 'ten stone'; or between the different roles a person may have: 'Madonna' and 'a mum'.

This analysis gives a model of the verb system that is useful for identifying ideological functions in texts. Verbs can be divided into two kinds, those that refer to actions – **actionals** – and those that refer to relations – **relationals** (see Hodge and Kress, 1993). Actional verbs can be divided into those that have an agent or actor who causes the action, and someone or something that is affected by the action (as, for example, in sentences 2 and 3 above). These verbs are called **transactives**. The other actional verbs – for example, 'went' – involve only the actor. There is no identifiable person or thing affected by the action. Verbs like this are called **non-transactives**.

actional $\left\{ \begin{array}{l} \text{Transactive (e.g., Alice installed the washer)} \\ \\ \text{non-transactive (e.g., She looked for the spanner)} \end{array} \right.$

Relational verbs can either represent the relationship between someone or something and a quality or attribute (as in sentence 1 above), or indicate an equal state between two nouns (as in sentences 5 and 6).

relational $\left\{ \begin{array}{l} \text{quality or attribute (e.g., That dog is vicious)} \\ \\ \text{equal state (e.g., David is my brother)} \end{array} \right.$

It is important to recognise that 'transactive' and 'non-transactive' don't mean the same as 'transitive' and 'intransitive'. To be transactive, a verb must represent an action that goes from the actor to the affected, as in 'Police arrested Paula Yates'. The label 'transitive' is applied to any verb that takes a direct object, so 'Mary is a teacher', 'David seems a bit of an oddity' are both transitive, but neither is transactive or even actional, but relational, representing an equal state.

By selecting from the range of models, the producer of text can present the world to the reader with an ideological slant imposed upon it. Are people or regimes presented as actors or recipients of action? Are they presented in terms of their behaviour or their qualities? The next section will look at some of the ways selection from the verb system can affect the ideological stance of the text.

MOTHERS BEHAVING BADLY: MADONNA AND MANDY ALLWOOD

As Unit 4 noted, women in news stories are frequently identified by a limited range of roles. This section will look at the way in which one of these roles is represented in the press.

The figure of the mother is a central one for British society in which Christianity may be seen as an important cultural influence. The image of the Madonna is so pervasive, that it was used as an advertising image for a Christmas 1996 recording company campaign (Virgin Records). An important aspect of this image is that this central Christian mother figure is also a virgin. The concept of the virgin mother neatly separates two aspects of life that are not necessarily separate: motherhood and sex.

Motherhood, and the role of the mother in our society, have, in the 1980s and 1990s, become a central issue for discussion – the single mother, the working mother, parenting skills, developments in fertility treatment are some of the issues that society has had to deal with. Motherhood tends to become newsworthy, though, when a story about an individual focuses the attention of the newspapers. The concept of motherhood and sexuality do not necessarily clash in the newspaper world when a woman celebrated for her beauty has a child (for example, p. 64), but a woman who aggressively markets her sexuality can be seen as flouting the cultural norm.

Women who go to extraordinary lengths to become mothers are generally praised by the newspapers. However, women who do this in a context that may be disapproved of – single women, women in unconventional relationships, for example – may be seen as operating against the norms of our society.

In 1996, two stories appeared that represented different aspects of women in the role of mothers. Madonna, the singer and actress, gave birth, an example of high-celebrity motherhood; and in this country, Mandy Allwood, a previously unknown woman conceived a multiple

79

pregnancy after taking fertility drugs, and attempted unsuccessfully to carry the pregnancy to full term.

Madonna has always been a controversial figure, challenging social norms by promoting both her sexuality and her independence. She does not represent, and does not appear to be planning to represent, the cultural image of the ideal mother. Mandy Allwood's story was initially greeted with enthusiasm by the papers that reported it - MIRACLE FOR MUM MANDY (*Sun*, 11 August 1996) - but when it was subsequently discovered that Ms Allwood was a divorced woman with one child, in a non-conventional relationship, with a partner who had two young children from another current relationship, was claiming state benefit, and had sold her story exclusively to one paper - then her status as an ideal mother quickly vanished.

Case study 1: Mandy Allwood

Activity

The following headline appeared on the front page of the *Sun* on 12 August 1996, the day after the story of Ms Allwood's pregnancy broke. The verb is actional and transactive. The someone or something affected by the action has been omitted. Complete the headline with something you think would be appropriate to the story.

I GOT --------------- FREE FROM BOOTS

Commentary

Knowing the details of the story, you probably put something like 'my prescription', or 'my fertility pills'. People who are not familiar with the story, or who don't know that this headline relates to it, suggest things such as 'my new glasses', 'some toothpaste', 'an extra pack of nappies'. The object of the verb 'got' in this context — that is, things that are 'got' from a major chain store — is expected to be some kind of commodity.

The actual headline was I GOT MY 8 BABIES FREE FROM BOOTS.

The following texts are articles that appeared on the front pages of the *Sun* and the *Independent* the day after the story of Ms Allwood's pregnancy broke in some Sunday newspapers.

◎ How is the relation between actor, action and affected used in these texts?

◎ How does this affect the reader's attitude to Ms Allwood?

Text: Octuplets

I GOT MY 8 BABIES FREE FROM *Boots*

GP's prescription for mum

By **ANDREW PARKER** and **JOHN ASKILL**

PREGNANT Mandy Allwood conceived her eight babies with a FREE prescription from Boots.

Mandy, 31, saw so desper-

EXCLUSIVE

ate to have a family by lover Paul Hudson she asked her GP for help.

The doctor put her on a seven-day course of NHS fertility

drugs – even though both she and Paul already had children.

Mandy took her prescription, worth £36, to her local Boots. She did not have to pay for it because she is a single mum on income support and exempt from ***Continued on Page Two***

Text: Mum

Million-pound mum

The mother who is expecting octuplets aims to make a million pounds through sponsorship deals and television commercials.

Commentary

The *Sun* and the *Independent* both use actional verbs with Ms Allwood as the actor. The *Sun* follows up its headline by focusing on all the steps Ms Allwood took to get pregnant – with the exception of the most crucial one. She 'conceived' the pregnancy, she 'asked' for help, 'took' her prescription to the chemist, 'did not have to pay'. Where these verbs are transactive, the affected relate to the children she hopes to have and the drugs she obtains. The overall effect is of someone operating independently – the involvement of the father of the children is minimised by the way the sentences are structured. Where he does appear, it is in the adjunct of a subordinate clause that links Ms Allwood with the quality of desperation via a relational verb:

> Mandy, 31, [relational verb] was [quality attributed to Ms Allwood] so desperate to have a family by lover Paul Hudson . . .

The *Independent* focuses on the financial aspects of the sale of the story, which it follows up with a longer article inside. The focus remains on Ms Allwood, who 'aims to make' a lot of money. This takes one aspect of the story further than the *Sun* does – it carries the implication that the point of the pregnancy is to make money.

Both these stories contain important social issues. The matters of fertility control, personal responsibility and possibly selling stories to newspapers in a way that can have consequences on subsequent events are all issues that require public debate. These stories as they appear, however, do not address these issues. They focus instead on the personal behaviour of one individual, and on issues that are not directly relevant to the story – Ms Allwood's receipt of free prescriptions, speculation about her motives for trying to take the pregnancy to full term. Both papers do address some of the issues either in editorials or in articles inside the paper, but readers of these may well have had their views influenced by the slant that the news articles have given to the story.

Activity

The following text is from the two-page spread that appeared inside the *Sun* on 12 August 1996. Several more participants have now been added to the story – apart from Mandy Allwood and Paul Hudson, the parents, there are Maria Edwards, who is the mother of Paul Hudson's two children, the police and Ms Allwood's parents – and the reader.

◎   How are actional and relational verbs used in relation to Mandy Allwood's parents and Maria Edwards?
◎   What actions are performed by each?
◎   What qualities are attributed to them?

Commentary

The article about Maria Edwards uses a lot of relational verbs in sentences where she is the subject and actor. She is discussed in terms of her qualities – she is 'mother to Paul's son', 'distraught', 'absolutely furious', 'stunned', very upset', 'in tears', 'too good for him', 'a lovely girl' and 'a great mum'. Where actional verbs are used, they often refer to mental processes, rather than 'cause and effect' relationships. Maria 'did not know', 'knew', 'heard'. The sentence 'She definitely has no intention of sharing Paul with Mandy' is interesting, as the verb 'intend' has been used in its **nominal** form, 'intention'. Therefore, instead of Maria Edwards' performing an action – 'intending' – she has a quality, or rather, the absence of a quality – 'no intention'. By depicting Maria Edwards largely in terms of her qualities – her emotions, her excellence as a mother, her devotion to her lover – she becomes very much the 'ideal woman', a passive victim.

Ms Allwood's parents are similarly represented by a large number of relational verbs, which again concentrates attention on their qualities and attributes. They are 'appalled and shocked'. Her mother is 'heartbroken'. The pattern of actional verbs in this section is interesting. In one case, the parents are the actors, and Ms Allwood is the person

83

Text: My Man

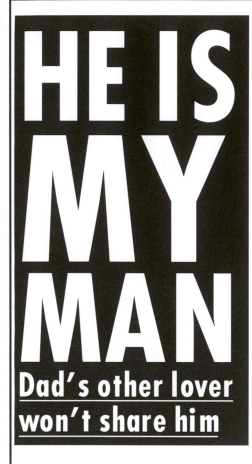

HE IS MY MAN

Dad's other lover won't share him

DO YOU KNOW MANDY OR PAUL?

IF YOU know Mandy Allwood or Paul Hudson, or any of their close relatives, call The Sun on 0171 782 4105. Don't worry about the cost — we'll call back.

By ANTONELLA LAZZERI

THE other lover of eight-babies dad Paul Hudson was "absolutely furious" last night — because she did not know he was regularly sleeping with Mandy Allwood.

A pal said pretty brunette Maria Edwards "regards Paul very much as her man." Maria, 28, who has two sons by Paul, was stunned at news of Mandy's multiple pregnancy.

The friend said: "She definitely has no intention of sharing Paul with Mandy – or anyone else for that matter. She knew Paul and Mandy were very close friends but thought that was because they had formerly been business partners.

"Until last week she knew nothing about any fertility treatment or that Mandy was expecting eight babies."

The pal said Maria "threw a fit" when she heard that Mandy expected to share Paul with her and that he would be dad to both families.

Maria's best friend Sheila McTurk said: "She's very upset. She was in tears when I saw her."

Diamonds

A neighbour in Hinckley, Leics, said Maria and Paul got engaged two years ago.

Welder Barry Cave, 38, said: "Maria made a big thing about coming over to our house to tell us.

"She showed us the ring with a small sapphire surrounded by diamonds. She was over the moon.

"I moved here five years ago and they have been together since then. Maria was madly in love with Paul, you could see that easily. But I wondered what was going on. Although he was here a lot he also used to go off to Birmingham to stop."

Unemployed Maria lives in a council semi with sons Zack, two, and seven-month-old Kane and a daughter from a previous relationship.

Builder Reg Green, 51, who lives next door, said: "Maria and Paul were practically living together.

"I've known Maria all her life, she's a lovely girl. I didn't really know him. I just thought he was a bit flash.

"He used to arrive in all these different expensive motors. I knew he was some kind of businessman and thought he must be well off. He and Maria seemed very much together and I used to see him playing with the kids. He was always very polite to me but not that chatty.

"I can't believe what he's done. More fool Maria if she stays with him. She's too good for him."

Another neighbour, pensioner Sue Hope, said: "I heard all about the mum expecting eight babies but never thought it had anything to do with Maria or Paul.

Children

"It's come as a hell of a shock. I've known Maria for years.

"She is a lovely girl and a great mum. Her children are perfectly turned-out and are really nice kiddies.

"I only know Paul to say hello to. I can't get over all this and don't know what's going to happen to Maria. I can't imagine she's happy."

A BMW stood outside Maria's home yesterday. There were toys and a child seat in the rear.

LOVER ❷

Mandy Allwood was Paul's business partner and is now expecting to have his eight babies

'QUIZ THEM' CALL TO COPS

By ANDREW PARKER

POLICE have been asked to investigate Mandy Allwood and lover Paul Hudson over alleged "dodgy" dealings in their property management company.

One flat owner claims she is owed £500 by the couple for rent she never received. Another client is after £300.

And a solicitor called in NatWest's fraud department after a cheque he sent to the pair was altered without his permission and channeled into Mandy's private account.

Property developer Paul, 37, declared himself bankrupt last year following the collapse of his business, Berkeswell Property Management Services, in Erdington, Birmingham.

Mandy was his office manager, working under her married name Pugh. After the crash of the firm they set up Richmond lettings three miles away.

Again they handled rented properties for owners, collected payments and kept an agreed percentage.

Paul has said he is now on income support after his second firm failed. But he and Mandy have left behind a trail of angry creditors.

One woman said: "I've built up a half-inch thick file on Hudson and Mandy Pugh, as I know her. Publicity over the babies gave me the shock of my life.

"When I read it I shouted out, 'That's them. I've got them'."

MANDY'S GP–Pages 4 and 5 ▬▬▬

Text: Daughter

She's no longer my daughter says mum

EXCLUSIVE
by JOHN ASKILL

MANDY'S heartbroken mother Marion said last night: "She is no longer my girl – I don't want to see her again."

Marion and husband Brian disowned Mandy because of her relationship with lover Paul Hudson.

And last night they were "appalled and shocked" by her decision to continue with the birth of the eight babies.

Marion, 58, said: "She has caused so much hurt. She had a good home and a loving family but she turned her back on us.

"As far as I am concerned, Mandy is not my daughter any more – she is somebody else.

Dumped

"I was not told she was even pregnant. The first I knew of it was when I saw it on TV."

The family was split after Mandy dumped husband Simon Pugh to begin a romance with Paul.

Brian, 60, blamed the split totally on Mandy's affair with Paul.

He said: "It's all about him. The divorce from Simon was very bitter. We had a terrible time. The whole episode has turned into a nightmare."

Ex-husband Simon's father branded Mandy a "moneygrabber" after she negotiated a deal to sell her story.

Andrew Pugh, 52, described his former daughter-in-law as an "extremely astute woman who is very ambitious."

affected: they 'disowned Mandy', and further in the article Ms Allwood is again the person affected by an action: her ex-father-in-law 'branded' her (a moneygrabber). Ms Allwood herself appears more often as the subject of a transactive verb: 'she caused . . . so much hurt', she 'dumped husband Simon Pugh' to 'begin a romance', she 'negotiated a deal'.

In contrast with these people, then, Mandy Allwood is depicted as someone who takes actions that affect the world around her, and affect it in a negative way.

DELETING THE ACTOR

In the example looked at in the activities above, the relationship between actor or agent, process and affected is considered. The choice of a transactive structure can focus the attention of the reader on the actor, and present a particular picture of an individual or group. In the above examples, Mandy Allwood frequently occupies the subject position in the clause, which places emphasis on her participation, often to the exclusion of others. However, a different effect is created if the actor is either placed in a less prominent position in the clause, or removed altogether.

English has the capacity to allow the rearrangement of **transitive** clauses so that the **direct object** of a verb becomes the grammatical subject. For example, the clause

| (subject) | (verb) | (direct object) |
| The dog | bit | the postman |

can be rewritten as:

| (subject) | (verb) | (agent phrase) |
| The postman | was bitten | by the dog |

The second structure, 'the postman was bitten by the dog', has the effect of putting more emphasis on the person or thing affected by the action and less on the actor, but also allows for the actor to be removed from the clause altogether:

The postman was bitten

Structures such as 'The dog bit the postman' are called **active**, or said to be in the **active voice**. Structures such as 'The postman was bitten by the dog' are said to be **passive** or in the **passive voice**.

87

Activity

Look at Text: Quiz on p. 85 again.

- ◎ Identify any passive structures.
- ◎ What effect do they create?

Commentary

The passive structures in this article are:

1 **Police have been asked to investigate** Mandy Allwood and lover Paul Hudson . . .
2 One flat owner claims **she is owed £500 by the couple** . . .
3 . . . after **a cheque he sent to the pair was altered** . . . and **channeled** into Mandy's private account.

By using a passive structure in the first sentence, the newspaper is able to focus on the fact that the police have been approached. The placing of the word 'police' in a prominent opening position gives a clear implication of criminal behaviour, which, in this context, it is difficult to dissociate from Mandy Allwood's pregnancy. The actor, in this case, has been deleted. The reader is not told who has asked the police to investigate and so is unable to tell how authoritative this call for an investigation is. The second use of passive structures in this article allows it to focus on the alleged victims of the '"dodgy" dealings'. The first allegation is clearly linked to Mandy Allwood: the actor is identified − 'by the couple', but in the case of the third passive, the second allegation, the actor is again deleted, leaving the reader to make the assumption that the actor is either Mandy Allwood or Mandy Allwood and Paul Hudson. By deleting the actor, the paper is able to imply illegal conduct without actually making an accusation that could leave them vulnerable to legal action. The actual content of the story has very little bearing on the news story − Mandy Allwood's multiple pregnancy.

Activity

The outcome of the pregnancy was, as predicted, unsuccessful. The births were premature, and the children did not survive.

- How are actional and relational verbs used in these articles to depict Mandy Allwood?
- How does this language use differ from the depiction of her in the earlier articles?

Text: Tears

MANDY'S TEARS FOR HER 8 TOTS

TRAGIC Mandy Allwood wept yesterday as her eight babies were laid to rest in white coffins 1ft long and 8ins deep.

She clung to partner Paul Hudson, 37, for support and whispered her farewells. The coffins had been laid on trestles shaped like teddy bears and rocking horses at a chapel in Norwood, South-East London.

Mandy 32 of Solihull, West Midlands. lost the octuplets — six boys and two girls — in the 19th week of pregnancy.

Text: Coffins

Eight miniature coffins put end to sad tale of Mandy Allwood pregnancy

MANDY Allwood's eight premature babies were buried in the same grave at West Norwood cemetery in south-east London yesterday.

Ms Allwood, aged 32, clung to her partner, Paul Hudson, in tears as they were lowered into the ground.

There were six boys and two girls, each in a white coffin one foot long. Blue posies on the coffins denoted the boys, with pink for the girls. The couple had written a message to each of the babies on cards laid in the wreaths placed next to the grave.

89

Commentary

As a bereaved mother, Mandy Allwood achieves the status of the ideal. The texts still use actional verbs, but these are now non-transactive. 'Tragic Mandy Allwood wept yesterday', 'she clung to her partner'. The verb 'clung' appears in both texts. The *Guardian* uses the adverb 'tearfully' rather than the verb 'wept'. The representation of Mandy Allwood as a woman who affects the world around her is now transformed into that of a woman who has been tragically affected herself by the world. Though it is easy to see the reasons for sympathising with Ms Allwood in this situation, it is difficult to account for the inconsistency in the representation of her in these articles compared to the earlier ones looked at above.

Summary

By conceiving a multiple pregnancy, Ms Allwood became the focus of a news story. The story developed, particularly in the tabloids, to turn Ms Allwood into a celebrity figure. All aspects of her life then became legitimate areas for the newspapers to target. The social issues relating to this story are not really addressed in the news articles that this analysis has looked at. Editorial comment does make some attempt to address these issues, but the news stories focus on personal aspects of the main characters, and particularly on Mandy Allwood herself. The depiction of her, rather than of the implications of her pregnancy, is consistently negative, and is frequently based on issues and events that have little or no bearing on the actual news – an octuple pregnancy.

Case study 2: Madonna

Activity

Text: Madonna baby appeared in the *Sun* on 15 October 1996.

- ◎ How is Madonna depicted in this article?
- ◎ What qualities does she have?
- ◎ What actions has she taken?

Text: Madonna baby

MADONNA BABY BORN

EXCLUSIVE

From CAROLINE GRAHAM in Los Angeles

SUPERSTAR Madonna gave birth to an "absolutely beautiful" girl last night.

The singer and her baby, believed to weigh 8lb, were both doing fine.

Madonna, 38, was whisked from her Hollywood home to the Good Samaritan Hospital, Los Angeles, when she went into labour four hours earlier.

She feared she would need a caesarian because of her age but a pal said: "She wanted a natural birth and got her way."

Madonna, star of new movie blockbuster Evita, was visited by lover Carlos Leon. They are tipped to name the child Lola.

A hospital source said: "Madonna is radiant and the baby absolutely beautiful."

Radiant . . new mum Madonna

Commentary

In this article, Madonna is represented as very much an 'ideal' mother. She is 'radiant'. The baby is 'absolutely beautiful', both are 'doing fine'. The verbs used, where actional, are more focused on mental processes than actions – Madonna 'feared', 'would need', 'wanted'. She is also the subject of a passive clause – 'Madonna was whisked from her Hollywood home ...' These representations of a celebrity mother are very much within the standard of the 'ideal' that newspapers depict. This article appeared very shortly after the birth, and is inaccurate in one important respect – Madonna's baby was in fact delivered by caesarean section.

FACTS AND POSSIBILITIES

Newspaper articles are ostensibly news stories - they report information. Editorials comment, speculate and give opinion. There is a third kind of article, however, the feature article, that falls between the two. The feature article picks up an item of news, and develops it via comment, opinion and speculation.

Text: Lourdes is an article that appeared in the *Daily Mail* the day after Madonna's baby was born. In this case, the image of the ideal mother is clearly not represented. The article presents Madonna as the kind of mother who will, in fact, be damaging for her child. Given that the baby is only one day old, and Madonna has no other children, where has the writer obtained the information on which to base her article? On close reading, it becomes apparent that this text gives very little factual material directly. It gives the information about the child's name, Lourdes Maria; it gives information about the birth - by caesarean section - but the main part of the content is opinion and speculation.

DELETING THE ACTION

The discussion about Mandy Allwood above looked at the way in which people involved in the story were said to have certain attributes or emotions, such as, for example, desperation or anger. These were presented to the reader through relational verbs: 'Mandy was so desperate', 'she [Maria Edwards]'s a lovely girl'. Sometimes, however, a writer can present a quality or attribute in the modifier of a noun phrase.

Activity

Is there any difference in meaning between the following sets of texts? The first pair are noun phrases taken from Text: Lourdes on p. 93; the second pair present the information contained in the noun phrases via a clause with a relational verb.

Set 1

◎ Her [Lourdes's] bizarre Christian name
◎ One of the most controversial, flamboyant, ambitious, self-obsessed women of modern times

Pity little Lourdes

Proud parents: But what kind of childhood will Madonna and Carlos give Lourdes?

PITY poor little Lourdes Maria, Madonna's newborn daughter. What sort of a childhood can she look forward to? Quite apart from her bizarre Christian name, she is the daughter of one of the most controversial, flamboyant, ambitious, self-obsessed women of modern times.

Even by the elastic moral standards of our day, Madonna has crossed almost every barrier. In her ruthless drive to amass a fortune by shamelessly purveying sex, she represents all the excesses of contemporary America.

Consider then the life facing little Lourdes. Madonna is probably sitting right now in a room so filled with flowers from the rich and famous vying for attention that little Lourdes is in danger of getting asthma from too much pollen inhalation.

Her mother, meanwhile, is already obsessed with getting back her figure after her convenient Caesarean section. She may once have taken the fashionable vow to breastfeed her newborn 'in order to fully comprehend the experience of childbirth' but she will probably realise quite quickly that is the quickest way to ruin the figure which has so far been her fortune.

No wonder Madonna is already looking for a nanny who knows how to fix a bottle. She reportedly wants an Englishwoman with her hair in a bun who speaks Spanish so the child can bond with its Spanish-speaking father, Carlos Leon, a fitness trainer.

But what if the father should find the state of unwedded bliss too demanding? Little Lourdes's mother may soon be looking for an English nanny with a bun who speaks German or French or Japanese, depending on who Madonna takes up with next.

by GLENYS ROBERTS

HOLLYWOOD children can rarely count on the same nanny or the same man being there throughout their childhood.

Hollywood parents are notorious for sacking the staff and their partners at the first sign of anything that threatens to undermine their ego. All in all, little Lourdes is quite likely to end up with just her extraordinary mother for company.

No matter, Madonna, the material girl, will reason: 'I can provide my daughter with everything she wants. I have always provided myself with everything I want and in more abundance than any man has been able to offer me.'

With money in the bank, a mixture of single-parent guilt and maternal pride will ensure little Lourdes never lacks the latest status symbol presents at Christmas and birthdays. The biggest status symbol of all, of course, is the child itself. By giving birth to her at the age of 38, Madonna, who usually likes to break new territory, is only following the latest fashion. These days, every actress over 40 is trying to conceive, while Mia Farrow is still adopting at the age of 52.

To be a status symbol means the child will have everything it wants but rarely anything it needs. A regular routine, discipline and the security of sleeping in the same bed at the same time each night may well prove more elusive than riches to the average child.

Little Lourdes will probably make her first public appearance at some fashionable restaurant while she is suckling at Madonna's breast, thus ensuring a photo to fascinate the world.

As soon as she can sit up, Lourdes will be strapped into a booster chair next to her mother, entertaining all her high-profile guests by repeatedly throwing her silver spoon on the floor.

Their adulation will give her the impression she was born to be the centre of attention and inspire a lot of temper tantrums if for one second she is not.

After the lunch and dinner parties will come the nightclub outings. A child as accoutrement can never be left at home. It must accompany the mother wherever she goes, rather like a Vuitton handbag.

Just look at what happened to Jane Birkin's daughter, Charlotte Gainsbourg. She went to her first nightclub at two and learned to sleep anywhere despite any number of decibels.

BY THE time she was in her teens, she had enough of it and had changed from an outgoing child into a sullen one. She now wants nothing more than a quiet life at home surrounded by close friends.

Chances are that little Lourdes will feel no different. By the time she is out of nappies, she will have seen both the low life and the high life. She will holiday in the best spots, fly first class, wear designer clothes and her godparents will be household names.

She will also have the obligatory Hollywood accessory, a psychiatrist — her mother does. The only thing she will not have had is a childhood.

But then Hollywood is littered with the casualties of the stars' roller-coaster lives. Only one Hollywood daughter has managed to survive the claustrophobia of famous parents and fulfil her potential. That is Jane Fonda — and even she had a rough ride. Her actress mother committed suicide.

Even Liza Minnelli with all her talent has not escaped the difficulties of being Judy Garland's daughter and has had constant battles with drug abuse. The list goes on and on.

And there's another matter to consider. While little Lourdes will never have anything in common with any other child because she has such a singular parent, the sadness is that many people will emulate Madonna.

They will never have her willpower or her earning power but, just like her, they will be able to conceive illegitimate children.

Of course, Madonna might just surprise us all and throw as much effort into being a good mother as she has into becoming one of the world's most famous women.

Alas, however, little Lourdes is more likely to grow up the unluckiest girl in the world.

MADONNA & CHILD
NEW SERIES STARTS ON PAGES 64-65

Set 2

◎   Lourdes Maria is a bizarre name
◎   Madonna is one of the most flamboyant, ambitious, self-obsessed women of modern times

Commentary

When an opinion is given via a clause with a relational verb, it is easier to recognise that an opinion has been offered. You might have responded to the sentences in set 2 by agreeing or disagreeing with them, or even withholding agreement or disagreement on the grounds that you have insufficient information to form an opinion. The texts in set 1, however, don't alert the reader to the fact that an opinion has been offered. The writer of the article has offered the view that 'Lourdes Maria' is a 'bizarre' name; and that Madonna is 'flamboyant, ambitious, self-obsessed'. The way this view is offered, however, conceals the fact that this is nothing more than opinion. There is, therefore, a difference in meaning between the texts in set 1 and the texts in set 2. Set 1 texts appear to refer to an accepted state of affairs, while set 2 texts offer an opinion that is open for discussion. By removing the relational verb, the writer can influence the opinion and ideological stance of the reader.

MODALITY

Modality refers to the way in which a text can express attitudes towards a situation, and is usually realised in the use of modal verbs (can, will, shall, may, must, could, would, should, might); and in the use of adverbs such as 'possibly', 'likely'.

Modal verbs carry a range of meanings, and it is a mistake to try to identify a fixed one-to-one relationship between verb and meaning; as is true of most aspects of language, context is vital to meaning. An important point to remember is that any action or process that is attached to a modal auxiliary has not necessarily happened. Look at the following examples:

He will go   he might go
he could have gone   he must go
he would have gone   he should go

In each case there is a degree of uncertainty about the status of the verb 'go'. It has not yet been performed and may not be, or it was not performed, or the fact of its performance is a matter of doubt. 'Will' is used in English as one way of expressing the future (English does not have an actual future tense form for the verb), and as such can have the force of prediction – this is likely to happen. 'Might', on the other hand, tends to imply that there is a strong possibility that the action or event won't, or didn't, take place (he might go, he might have gone).

Activity

Read Text: Lourdes again. Identify the modal verbs and adverbs. What degree of probability do these suggest to you as a reader?

Commentary

The modal auxiliaries in this article express a range of probabilities – predictions that are likely to happen: '[Madonna] **will** . . . realise quite quickly that [breast feeding] is the quickest way to ruin the figure'; 'a mixture of single-parent guilt and maternal pride **will** ensure little Lourdes never lacks the latest status symbol presents'; 'Little Lourdes **will** . . . make her first public appearance at some fashionable restaurant'; 'Lourdes **will** be strapped into a booster chair'; events that are strong possibilities: 'Little Lourdes's mother **may** soon be looking for an English nanny'; '. . . routine, . . . discipline and . . . security **may** prove more elusive'. All of these present Madonna as an unsatisfactory mother. Towards the end of the article, the possibility that these speculations could be incorrect is conceded: 'Madonna **might** just surprise us'; however, the modal auxiliary chosen is one that implies that this is unlikely.

The predictions are backed up by the use of adverbs that carry the meaning of strong probability: 'probably', 'likely'.

The use of modal verbs, and the choice of adverbs, allow the writer to present opinion and speculation about Madonna in a way that gives it almost the status of fact.

Activity

Read the text again, and answer the following questions:

◎ How does the article interact with the reader? You might want to look at direct address, the use of questions and imperatives, and assumptions of shared views.

◎ Does this interaction affect the ideological stance of the text?

95

Commentary

The writer does not use direct address in the sense of naming the reader – there is no use of 'you', or even *Daily Mail* readers'. There is also no named implied audience – no 'law-abiding people'. There is, though, a group being addressed – the 'our' of 'our day', the 'us' in 'Madonna might just surprise us all'. The actual reader of the text may, as noted above, disagree with some of the opinions expressed in the article, but the implied reader, the 'us', is apparently in agreement.

The writer also selects interrogative and imperative structures, and uses a series of questions and instructions to address this audience. The questions imply a shared viewpoint with the reader. 'What sort of a . . .' as a question opening tends to imply a critical meaning. 'What sort of a childhood can she look forward to?' carries the implication that her childhood will be bad, particularly in the context of this article. Questions also evoke a response. The reader will respond with 'Yes, what sort of a childhood . . . ?' Similarly, the wording of the question 'But what if the father should find the state of unwedded bliss too demanding?' implies that this is what will happen. The phrase 'unwedded bliss' carries strong negative connotations, and the contrast between 'bliss' and 'too demanding' gives the question an ironic tone that limits the reader's potential responses.

The use of imperative structures also helps to direct the reader's opinion. At the opening of the article, we are invited, in fact directed, to 'pity' Madonna's child, and the pattern of imperatives directs the reader to take a series of actions or stances in relation to a series of opinions that are being presented via language that is strongly emotionally loaded.

PUTTING IT IN ORDER

The discussion above on the articles about Mandy Allwood looked at the way in which the relationship between the actor and the verb could be manipulated to create a particular emphasis or focus. One of the ways in which this was done was by the use of passive structures ('Police have been asked to investigate') that bring to the front of the sentence something that would not otherwise have been there. The **unmarked**, or expected, order of clause elements is **subject, verb, object, complement** and **adjunct** or **adverbial**.

Look again at the first three paragraphs of Text: Lourdes.

◎ Does the sentence begin with the subject of the clause, or with another clause element?
◎ What is the effect of deviating from the unmarked order?

Commentary

The **theme** of a clause – its topic or most emphasised element – is the first complete word unit. In declarative clauses, this is usually the grammatical subject. Any other element in this position is given emphasis by its placing – it is what the sentence is about, or the aspect of the information that the speaker or writer wants to give prominence to. In this article, there are three different kinds of emphasis given by the reordering of clause elements:

1   The use of imperatives brings the verb to the front, thus the article opens on the strongly emotive word 'pity'.

2   Questions bring either an auxiliary verb to the front, or a wh-word (what, where, who, when, how). The fronting of the wh-word 'what' makes the reader start to ask the question before he or she knows what is being asked.

3   The adjunct, or adverbial element of the clause, usually appears at the end of the clause in its expected or unmarked position. However, it can appear at almost any place in the clause, depending on what emphasis the writer wants to give it. In two of these sentences, the adjunct appears first: 'even by the elastic moral standards of our day'; 'in her ruthless drive to amass a fortune by shamelessly purveying sex'. This fronting of the adjunct has the effect of emphasising the material contained in it, but also of discouraging the reader from querying the opinion contained in it as he/she needs to read on quickly to make sense of the sentence. The fronting of 'Quite apart from her bizarre Christian name' has a similar effect, though this is not, in fact, an adjunct of this clause as it bears no relation to the verb.

Summary

There are a range of choices that a writer can make at the level of syntax that can evoke different responses in the reader. The ones looked at in this unit are not the only ones available to the writer, but they are some of the most commonly used: selection from the verb system; relation between actor and action, including the use of passive structures; modality; use of imperative and interrogative structures, and the reorganisation of clause units to make different elements of the clause the theme of the sentence.

Extension

1   Analyse a selection of news reports and feature articles that you think present an ideologically biased representation of an item of news. Do news reports and feature articles use the same language devices, or is there an identifiable difference?

2   Collect news reports, editorials and feature articles that relate to the same story from one newspaper. How is the ideological stance of the paper maintained across this range?

3   Compare a similar collection across a range of newspapers. How are different ideological stances represented and maintained?

Discourse

Texts form coherent units of language that are constructed to operate in units larger than the single sentence or utterance. This section will look at the way newspaper texts form a coherent whole, carrying a clear ideological stance throughout an article. The previous units have looked at aspects of lexis – the vocabulary choices that a writer makes – and aspects of syntax, and the way these levels of language can operate in newspaper texts. Lexical and syntactic patterns are an important aspect of discourse – for example, the patterns of word choice identified in Unit 4, and the patterns of modality identified in the article about Madonna (p. 93), help to make the text form a coherent unit.

Texts have been selected in the previous two units because they demonstrate the way in which specific groups are represented in the language of newspapers. This section will look at representations of a group that is foregrounded because of a political event – a war – and which in this context is a legitimised target for newspaper comment, being both hostile and non-British.

JOHNNY FOREIGNER: NEWSPAPERS AT WAR

In 1982, Argentina invaded the Falkland Islands which, though they are on the other side of the world, are British territory. The Argentinian government, prior to this event, was not seen as hostile, rather the opposite, having been a customer of the British arms industry – despite a worrying human-rights record. The British government, at that time unpopular at home, launched a Task Force to retake the islands. The threat of force, and its subsequent use, was not fully supported by all political wings in Britain, or by the United Nations, as it was believed that the situation could have been resolved by negotiation. There was, therefore, a clear ideological division of opinion on this matter, and there were issues that demanded serious and informed debate. This section looks at the way this event was depicted in the newspapers at the time, and the way in which patterns of cohesion can help to reinforce the ideological 'message' of the text.

IDENTIFYING PATTERNS IN TEXT

Activity

The following text consists of sentences taken in random order from two articles that appeared in the *Times* and the *Sun* on 4 May 1982. They report the attack on the Argentine cruiser the *General Belgrano*. The headline of the *Times* article is ARGENTINE CRUISER HIT BY TORPEDOES FROM ROYAL NAVY SUBMARINE, and the headline from the *Sun* is GOTCHA. The sentences have been mixed together. Try to reconstruct the two articles; then check your answer by looking at the original articles at the end of the unit. The article from the *Sun* is not complete, only the first eight paragraphs are used.

◎ What language features helped you to separate the texts?
◎ What language features helped you to put the texts into the correct order?
◎ If you reconstructed the texts wrongly, what language features misled you?

Text

1   The General Belgrano is a 13,644-ton cruiser carrying helicopters and Seacat missiles.

2   The Belgrano, which survived the Pearl Harbour attack when it belonged to the US Navy, had been asking for trouble all day.

3   The Argentine cruiser General Belgrano was hit last night by torpedoes fired from a British submarine, the Ministry of Defence said earlier today.

4   The Navy had the Argies on their knees last night after a devastating double punch.

5   The cruiser was believed to be severely damaged; the submarine was undamaged and had resumed patrol.

6   WALLOP: They torpedoed the 14,000-ton Argentine cruiser General Belgrano and left it a useless wreck.

7   The cruiser had posed a significant threat to the British task force the ministry said.

8   With its 15 six-inch guns our Navy high command were certain that it would have played a major part in any battle to retain the Falklands.

9   But the Belgrano and its 1,000 crew needn't worry about the war for some time now.

10 The action, at about 8pm British time, was said to be fully in accordance with the instructions given to the task force commander based upon the right of self defence under Article 51 of the United Nations charter.

11 The cruiser, second largest in the Argy fleet, had been skirting the 200-mile war zone that Britain has set up around the Falkland Islands.

12 For the nuclear submarine Conqueror, captained by Commander Richard Wraith, let fly with two torpedoes.

13 WALLOP: Task Force helicopters sank one Argentine patrol boat and severely damaged another.

Commentary

You will probably find that you separated the texts with a reasonable degree of success, and managed to reconstruct the originals without too many mistakes. The reason for this is that each text has distinctive

101

patterns running through it that help the reader to identify a specific text, and pinpoint the way the material within each text is sequenced.

LEXICAL COHESION

One of the patterns you will have identified and used is the pattern that exists within the words and phrases of a text. This is called **lexical cohesion.** Some of the patterns that exist within the texts are:

Semantic field (the use of words and phrases from a particular area of meaning)

Both articles use words from the semantic field of war. The *Sun* also uses the language of boxing, or perhaps brawling: 'a devastating double punch', 'wallop', 'asking for trouble', 'let fly'.

The *Times* uses the language of politics and international law: 'The Ministry of Defence', 'Article 51 of the United Nations Charter'.

Direct repetition (the same word repeated)

> *Sun*: 'wallop', 'wallop'
> *Times*: 'the Ministry . . . said', 'the Ministry said'

Synonyms (words with very similar meanings)

> *Sun*: 'punch', 'wallop'
> *Times*: 'was hit', 'severely damaged'

Antonyms (opposites)

> *Times*: 'damaged', 'undamaged'

Specific to general reference (where the same thing is referred to, but the first reference has more detail)

> *Times*: 'The 14,000-ton Argentina cruiser General Belgrano', 'the cruiser', 'it'
> *Sun*: 'The Argentine cruiser General Belgrano', 'the cruiser', 'the General Belgrano'

Level of formality (texts can use different levels of formality to address a specific topic)

> Formal (*Times*): 'fully in accordance with', 'severely damaged', 'posed a significant threat'
> Informal (*Sun*): 'Argies', 'a useless wreck', 'asking for trouble'

The patterns of word choice in the text carry a clear ideological 'message'. The *Sun* represents the war as a brawl or a scrap, in which one of the participants had been 'asking for trouble', and had received a well-deserved hit. The *Times* represents the war as a serious, formal event that operates – on the British side – within the rules of law.

GRAMMATICAL COHESION

This unit has already discussed briefly some of the patterns of grammatical cohesion that occurred in texts used in the previous unit – patterns of modality, for example. This section will identify some other patterns of grammatical cohesion that will have helped you to identify and reconstruct the texts in this activity.

REFERENCE

Pronouns

Neither text uses many pronouns – they are both explicit in their use of nouns. They both use the pattern 'the General Belgrano . . . it', though this occurs only once in the *Times*, and the *Sun* uses 'The Navy . . . they'.

Definiteness

This refers to the use of definite and indefinite determiners. New information is frequently signalled by the use of the indefinite article 'a', information already held by the reader is signalled by the definite article 'the'. The *Times* uses 'the' to introduce the Belgrano, but this is because it is identified by a proper noun – there is only one General Belgrano. The submarine that attacked it, however, is '**a** British submarine'. This clearly indicates that the task force has the resources of several submarines, as well as allowing the reader to follow a pattern through the text. The next reference is '**the** submarine'. The *Sun* uses the definite form for both vessels consistently through the article.

103

Reference outside the text: exophoric reference

All the information contained in the use of pronouns and articles is contained within the text - though the *Sun's* consistent use of the definite form implies a shared knowledge with the reader that may not actually exist. This reader who shares knowledge and experience with the *Sun* is found again in the use of possessive pronouns as determiners in noun phrases. 'Our lads', 'our Navy', 'our super nuclear sub'. This is an address to the reader who is outside the text. This reader is clearly in agreement with the war as it is reported, and familiar with the details of engagement. This exophoric reference helps to create the implied reader who is addressed by this text (see Unit 2).

Another form of exophoric reference in these texts occurs in the use of deictic reference (p. 26). The picture captions in the *Sun* article use deictic reference - 'like **this** one' needs the picture to make sense.

The *Times* uses almost no exophoric reference, apart from time references: 'last night' (also used in the *Sun*) and 'today'. These are only appropriate to the day the articles appeared. To the later reader, 'last night' and 'today' carries no direct reference.

Links between sentences: conjunctions

Sentences frequently refer back to the previous sentence or forward to the next when an argument or discussion is being developed. In the *Sun* article, the Belgrano is conditionally presented as a threat to the task force - it 'would have played a major part'. This use of the modal 'would' leads the reader to expect a condition or qualification that follows with the conjunction 'but' at the beginning of the following sentence. The modal 'needn't' in this sentence again leads the reader to expect reason or consequence, which again is provided at the beginning of the next sentence - 'For'.

The *Times* article links its sentences by sequencing in time - 'last night', 'early today', 'at about 8pm', and by the use of specific to general reference (p. 102 above).

Sentence type

Unit 5 above looked at the use of imperative and interrogative sentences in a newspaper text. The *Sun* article 'Gotcha' uses another sentence type, the exclamation. Exclamations create a sense of emotion or excitement that is shared by the reader, thus 'Gotcha', 'Wallop' (repeated twice) encourages the reader to join the sense of triumphalism that the article engenders.

These sentences are also grammatically incomplete – 'Gotcha' has no subject, and 'Wallop' lacks a grammatical context (it is impossible to tell whether this is a verb or a noun). Sentences like these are called **minor sentences**, and are a feature of spoken language. By using these forms the *Sun*, as well as creating a sense of excitement, gives a 'speech-like' effect. If the writer of the article is speaking directly to the reader, or the implied reader, this, perhaps, has the effect of 'cheering on' one side in a brawl.

The *Times* uses declarative sentences, the form most often associated with the delivery of information. This accords well with the rather weighty, formal tone that the *Times* adopts, and helps to give the content of the article the status of verifiable fact.

Verbs

The use of verbs within a text can establish important points relating to time, and to the relationship between actor, process and affected, in the use of active or passive voice (Unit 5).

The verbs used in both texts are mostly in the past tense – a form often found in narrative fiction, used to recount events that have already happened. The *Times* uses some passive structures – 'The Argentine cruiser ... was hit'; 'the cruiser was believed to be ...'; 'The action ..... was said to be ...' The *Sun* uses active forms, and a lot of transactive verbs for the actions of the British: 'They torpedoed the 14,000-ton ... cruiser'; 'Task force helicopters sank one Argentine patrol boat'.

The *Times*' use of passives helps to give the article the level of formality required by the approach it takes to the story, and also has the effect of distancing or removing the actor from the events. The *Sun* represents the British navy as active participants in a fight they didn't start, but are winning.

Summary

The patterns of lexical and grammatical cohesion identified in these texts not only help them to form complete, coherent units, but also allow the ideological approaches of the texts to develop coherently. The *Sun* adopts a 'gung-ho' approach that is enhanced by its patterns of informality, its use of terms appropriate to brawling or fist-fighting, its appeal to shared beliefs and the implication of danger or threat averted in its use of would have ... but ... for patterns.

The *Times* adopts a more formal, low-key approach, in its use of

105

more formal language, its more impersonal reference and its appeal to legal statutes.

Narrative in newspaper texts

WHAT IS NARRATIVE?

Narrative is story-telling. It can be described as the retelling of past experiences in which language recreates past events into a narrative sequence; these narratives are usually recognised as recounting real events. Narrative can also be described as the telling of a sequence of events that are not directly or closely related to past experience. These narratives are usually recognised as fictional.

Narrative of both kinds have identifiable structures. William Labov, in his study of the language of the New York black community, analysed the oral narrative of pre-teenagers, adolescents and adults, and identified patterns that occurred across a range of narratives that his informants used to recount events in their lives. These narratives recounted the experience in temporal sequence, matching the order of the narrated events. Labov also identified other elements in the structure of these narratives. He claimed that a fully formed narrative may show the following structure:

1 **Abstract** – a brief summary of the whole story
2 **Orientation** – the time, the place, the people, the situation
3 **Complicating action** – the content or events of the narrative
4 **Evaluation** – an indication of the point of the narrative
5 **Result or resolution** – the termination of the series of events
6 **Coda** – a summing up that signals the end of the narrative

In Unit 1, newspaper stories were compared with other kinds of texts, and found to have language patterns in common with narrative fiction. As has already been discussed, news reports are frequently referred to as stories. To what extent do news articles follow patterns of narrative?

Activity

Look again at the *Sun* article 'Gotcha'. Can you identify the patterns of narrative that Labov identifies? You should look for:

- A brief summary at the beginning
- Information about the circumstances – the time, the place, the people, the situation
- A sequence of events
- The point of, or the reason for telling, the story
- The end of the sequence of events
- A summing up

Commentary

The article follows the structure that Labov identifies quite closely. The headline forms an abstract – it summarises the events of the story. The circumstances are outlined in the first paragraph. The reader is given information about the people 'the navy', 'the Argies' and the time 'last night', though an important point here is that the people are largely absent – there are ships, helicopters and navies, but very few actual people are mentioned. The place and circumstances are contained in the logo that appears next to the first three paragraphs 'Battle for the Falklands' and a picture of a soldier running into battle. The events are clearly sequenced by the use of verb tense and conjunctions that relate the events either temporally or as cause and effect. The evaluation is not so easy to identify. This story does not really need a reason – its content tells the reader that it is important. There is some evaluation contained in the description of the Belgrano – this emphasises the threat the cruiser was supposed to represent to the British navy and thus the importance of the story. The end of the sequence is marked by the final paragraph. There is no summing up or coda, but the full article is not reproduced.

Summary

This unit has looked at some of the devices that operate to make newspaper texts coherent and cohesive. These devices: patterns of word choice, patterns of syntax operate to make the text a complete unit at the level of structure and at the level of meaning. Patterns of word choice and syntax can carry an ideological slant through a text, establish a relationship with the audience; and establish the nature of that audience, in the sense that newspapers often address an implied audience rather than an actual one.

Newspaper texts may also carry larger patterns. The analysis at the end of the unit demonstrates the way in which a news story follows closely patterns identified for narrative. These patterns give the text cohesion and coherence, but may also put the reader in the role of the reader of narrative, rather than the reader of news. In recent years compassion fatigue has been identified as a feature of our society, when people apparently lose interest in the welfare of victims of the disasters that happen around the world. The audience for news stories apparently gets bored with a war, a famine, the victims of an oppressive regime. Maybe that is because these are represented to us as stories – and we are ready for new ones.

Text: Cruiser

Argentine cruiser hit by torpedoes from Royal Navy submarine

● The Argentine cruiser General Belgrano was hit last night by torpedoes fired from a British submarine, the Ministry of Defence said early today. The cruiser was believed to be severely damaged; the submarine was undamaged and had resumed patrol. The cruiser had posed a significant threat to the British task force the ministry said. The action, at about 8 pm British time, was said to be fully in accordance with the instructions given to the task force commander based upon the right of self defence under Article 51 of the United Nations Charter. The General Belgrano is a 13,644-ton cruiser carrying helicopters and Seacat missiles. It was commissioned in 1939.

● An offer by Mrs Thatcher for all-party talks at Westminster on the crisis was rejected yesterday by Mr Michael Foot.

By Philip Webster, Political Reporter

GOTCHA

Our lads sink gunboat and hole cruiser

BATTLE FOR THE ISLANDS

From TONY SNOW aboard HMS Invincible

THE NAVY had the Argies on their knees last night after a devastating double punch.

WALLOP: They torpedoed the 14,000-ton Argentina cruiser General Belgrano and left it a useless wreck.

WALLOP: Task Force helicopters sank one Argentine patrol boat and severely damaged another.

The Belgrano, which survived the Pearl Harbour attack when it belonged to the U.S. Navy, had been asking for trouble all day.

The cruiser, second largest in the Argy fleet, had been skirting the 200-mile war zone that Britain has set up around the Falkland Islands.

MAJOR

With its 15 six-inch guns our Navy high command were certain that it would have played a major part in any battle to retain the Falklands.

But the Belgrano and its 1,000 crew needn't worry about the war for some time now.

For the nuclear submarine Conqueror, captained by Commander Richard Wraith, let fly with two torpedoes.

The ship was not sunk and it is not clear how many casualties there were.

Extension

1   This unit has looked at cohesive devices in a limited range of newspaper texts. Do all newspapers follow similar patterns? Do a comparison of stories across different types of newspaper — broadsheet and tabloid; local and national are two possible comparisons — and see if these papers use the same devices to construct and maintain a particular type of discourse.

2   Can you identify patterns of narrative in news stories across the range of newspapers? Is this a feature of broadsheet as well as tabloid journalism?

3   The following text is an editorial from the American newspaper *USA Today*. Does this text use the language devices identified through this book to create an ideological stance?

Today's topic: GRADE INFLATION

When everyone gets an A, grades are meaningless

OUR VIEW High school seniors applying for college find that an A average isn't what it used to be.

An A average no longer makes the grade in college placements. Just ask high school "honor" students.

Rather than heading to elite colleges, some academic all-stars are collecting rejection slips. The reason: more A-average students than ever before applying to college.

Studies by UCLA — where high school seniors with 4.3 grade-point averages often are rejected — show that 31.5% of college freshmen nationwide last fall reported average grades of A- or higher. That's up from 22.6% in 1990 and twice the level 30 years ago. Only one-fourth of college applicants average less than a B, down from 35% in 1990 and 45% in 1966.

Are today's college-bound students that much brighter or harder working than their predecessors?

Obviously not. College entrance exams aren't improving. For A students entering college, SAT scores have actually dropped several points in the past decade.

What's going on is not improved scholarship but rather inflated grading.

A U.S. Department of Education study found A's and B's in many urban schools are no better than C's and D's. Districts pump up grades for non-academic achievements, from class attendance to community service. And more than half of all school districts now weight grades, awarding bonus points for taking college prep classes.

The goal of such weighting is laudable: to reward kids for tackling tougher courses.

But the bonus-point systems differ wildly. Atlanta uses a 6-point scale. Other districts, a 5. Still others simply add a half point. And there's no consistency from district to district on which courses qualify.

Because this mishmash makes GPAs almost meaningless to college admissions offices, many are putting more weight on college admissions tests, like the SAT.

Those tests, though, give an edge to students with access to special classes on how to take them. Worse, results come too late for students or their parents to do much to improve skills to succeed in college.

Already, more than a quarter of college entrants need tutoring or remedial courses in math, one in eight in English. Catching up wastes time and money. Many college students now take a year or more to finish college than 20 years ago. And that extra year can cost an average of $7,000 at a public college, $18,000 at a private school.

What's the answer?

Some schools ditch grades altogether, relying on teacher evaluations and portfolios of students' work. But college admissions officers say portfolios soon become a blur, and evaluations must be translated into grades to compare with other applicants.

Admissions officers prefer a nationally standardized system for weighting grades. But getting all schools to agree on a standard would be difficult if not impossible.

A different approach with promise is under way at the University of Washington. Each year, grades of its students are compared with their high school records. The differences between high school GPAs and college GPAs are published each fall, giving both parents and students an assessment of their high school's grading system.

Another remedy allows students to take tougher courses to earn class honors but gives them no extra grade points. Most college admissions offices already weight grades for advanced courses on their own, so students who take on the challenge would lose no advantage in college admissions.

High school grades should mean what they say. That's the best way to give students and parents an accurate picture of what's possible in college.

Earning college credit

According to the College Board, more than 200,000 high school grads this year will start college with credits earned in high school, which can add to grade confusion. Percentage of schools participating in the advanced placement program compared with 1987:

	% in '96	Change from '87
Alabama	45	7
Alaska	12	-3
Arizona	57	11
Arkansas	27	14
California	69	15
Colorado	50	15
Connecticut	84	25
Delaware	46	-4
Dist. of Columbia	100	61
Florida	57	9
Georgia	59	25
Hawaii	68	20
Idaho	39	16
Illinois	50	22
Indiana	55	22
Iowa	29	20
Kansas	24	13
Kentucky	62	31
Louisiana	24	10
Maine	58	19
Maryland	71	10
Massachusetts	80	28
Michigan	52	17
Minnesota	44	26
Mississippi	38	26
Missouri	26	14
Montana	31	17
Nebraska	19	8
Nevada	56	20
New Hampshire	68	17
New Jersey	85	26
New Mexico	42	24
New York	72	18
North Carolina	64	23
North Dakota	7	5
Ohio	58	20
Oklahoma	16	7
Oregon	44	9
Pennsylvania	60	20
Rhode Island	74	25
South Carolina	70	20
South Dakota	14	10
Tennessee	50	20
Texas	51	31
Utah	70	10
Vermont	66	24
Virginia	70	16
Washington	53	10
West Virginia	63	44
Wisconsin	57	40
Wyoming	30	17
Total U.S.	52	19

index of terms

This is a form of combined glossary and index. Listed below are some of the main key terms used in the book, together with brief definitions for purposes of reference. The page references will normally take you to the first use of the term in the book, where it will be usually shown in **bold**. In some cases, however, understanding of the term can be helped by exploring its uses in more than one place in the book, and accordingly more than one page reference is given.

actional   78
Verbs that refer to processes that can be defined as actions. The actional model can be divided into two kinds – transactive and non-transactive. A transactive verb is a verb in which the action passes from the actor/agent to the affected. A non-transactive verb is one that refers to an action or process in which there is one entity related to a process. The entity can't easily be classified as actor/agent or affected. For example in the sentence 'The boy runs', the boy is both performing the action and affected by it. This model is a simplified version of the one given by Hodge and Kress (1979).

active (see **voice**)

adjunct   (see **adverbial**)

adverbial   96
That part of the clause that carries information about place, manner, time, frequency, degree, cause, etc. It can be an adverb, an adverb phrase or an adverb clause e.g. 'Madonna gave birth ------ last night.'.

agent phrase   (see **voice**)

cohesion   102
The pattern of language created within a text, mainly within and across sentence boundaries, and which collectively make up the organisation of larger units of text such as paragraphs. Cohesion can be both lexical and grammatical. Lexical cohesion is established by means of chains of words of related meaning linking across sentences; grammatical cohesion is established by grammatical words – the, this, it, etc.

connotation   18
The associations a word creates.

deictic   26
Deictic words point out or specify a time, a place, a person, a thing. Deictics can point in various directions, both within the text and outside it.

exophoric   104
Reference outside the text.

grammatical cohesion   (see **cohesion**)

grammatical word   19
A word that carries a grammatical rather than a semantic meaning, for example determiners, auxiliary verbs.

graphology   55
The visual aspects of text, including layout and images.

homophones 17
Words that have the same pronunciation but differ in meaning, for example roll, role.

homonym 17
A word that has more than one meaning, meanings that are not closely related, e.g. Lighter = less heavy, lighter = a device for lighting cigarettes.

intertextuality 18
The way in which a text echoes or refers to another text, e.g. the phrase 'the bloom with a phew' refers to the title of E.M. Forster's novel *A Room With a View*.

lexical cohesion (see **cohesion**)

lexical word 19
A word that carries full semantic meaning.

minor sentence 105
A sentence that does not contain all the features of a full sentence, often found in spoken language.

modality 94
The way in which a text can express an attitude towards a situation, usually through the use of modal verbs (see **modal verb**) and adverbs such as 'probably', 'certainly' or constructions such as 'it is certain that ...'.

modal verb 94
A verb used to express modality, for example 'must', 'can', 'could', 'will', 'would', 'shall', 'may'.

modifier 21
Premodifier, post-modifier (see **noun phrase**).

nominalisation 83
The process of forming a noun from another part of speech, by the addition of an appropriate

suffix, for example accept + ance = acceptance.

non-transactive 78
An actional structure in which there is only one actor or entity and there is no easily identified actor or affected, e.g. 'The boy runs', 'John played tennis'. (see **actional**)

noun phrase 20
A word or group of words with a noun as its head (essential word), with added information or detail in the form of modifiers. Premodifiers come before the head, post-modifiers follow it. Noun phrases have the possible structure of 'determiner', 'premodifier', 'headword' (noun or pronoun), 'post-modifier'. For example, 'he'; 'the strange boy'; 'the strange boy in blue shoes'; are all noun phrases.

passive (see **voice**)

phonological 55
Relating to the sound system of the language. Some phonological devices texts can use are alliteration - the repetition of an initial sound - and phoneme substitution - the replacement of an expected sound by an unexpected one ('hit and myth', rather than 'hit and miss').

phrasal verb 20
A verb followed by a particle (usually a preposition) that together have a specific and independent meaning.

polyseme 18
A word that has two or more closely related meanings, for example 'head' can mean 'part of the body', 'person in charge', 'front of the line', etc.

pragmatics 41

The factors that govern the choice of language in social interaction, and the effects those choices have.

relational 78

Verbs that involve the relationship between two entities or between an entity and a quality.

semantic field 71

A group of words that are related in meaning, normally as a result of being connected with a particular context of use, for example 'storm', 'thunder', 'rain', 'hail' all belong to the semantic field of weather.

syntax 77

The relationships between elements in a clause.

theme 97

The theme of a clause is usually the first main word unit of a sentence.

transactive 78

A structure in which the action passes from the actor to the affected, e.g. 'The boy hit the ball'. (see **actional**)

transitive 87

The relationship between the verb or verb group, the participants in the action, state or process and other elements of the clause.

vocative 31

Nouns or noun phrases used to denote the person who is directly addressed, e.g. '**John**, close the window'.

voice 87

A grammatical feature which indicates whether the subject in a sentence is the agent of an action or is affected by the action. Voice can be either active or passive, for example: 'The girl threw the ball' (active); 'The ball was thrown by the girl' (passive). The passive voice allows the agent phrase, that is the 'by'- phrase, to be deleted: 'The ball was thrown'.

index of main texts

further reading

Fowler, Roger (1991) *Language in the News: Discourse and Ideology in the Press*, Routledge, London.

—— Hodge, Bob, Kress, Gunther and Trew, Tony (1979) *Language and Control*, Routledge, London.

Hartley, John (1982) *Understanding News*, Routledge, London.

Herman, Edward S. and Chomsky, Noam (1988) *Manufacturing Consent: The Political Economy of the Mass Media*, Random House, New York.

Mills, Sarah (1995) *Feminist Stylistics*, Routledge, London.

Simpson, Paul (1993) *Language, Ideology and Point of View*, Routledge, London.

references

Hodge, Robert and Kress, Gunther (1993) *Language as Ideology*, 2nd edn, Routledge, London.

Labov, William (1997) *Language in the Inner City: Studies in the Black English Vernacular*, Blackwell, Oxford.

Tunstall, Jeremy (1996) *Newspaper Power: The New National Press in Britain*, Clarendon Press, Oxford.